You, The Jury II

You, The Jury II

©2018 Charles H. Helein.
©2018 Belle Louve Corporation.
All Rights Reserved. No part of this publication may be reproduced, stored in a retrieval system or transmitted in any form by any means electronic, mechanical, or photocopying, recording or otherwise without the permission of the author.

Printed in the United States

YOU, THE JURY II

H. H. CHARLES

CONTENTS

FOREWORD
In The Circuit Court Of The Commonwealth Of Virginia
In And For Loudoun County.. 1

CHAPTER 1
"Hear Ye, Hear Ye"... 5

CHAPTER 2
Autopsy... 8

CHAPTER 3
Witness For The Prosecution: Paul Engel 16

CHAPTER 4
Witness For The Prosecution: Detective Keith Thornton 42

CHAPTER 5
Witness For The Prosecution: Ray Gotti... 69

CHAPTER 6
Witness For The Defense: Carl Truitt 82

CHAPTER 7
Witness For The Defense: Joey Lee 104

CHAPTER 8
Witness For The Defense: Brian Grant 113

CHAPTER 9
Closing Arguments: Jury Instructions 124

CHAPTER 10
Jury Deliberations 137

ABOUT THE AUTHOR 149

FOREWORD

INDICTMENT

In The Circuit Court Of The Commonwealth Of Virginia In And For Loudoun County

Commonwealth Of Virginia v. Carl L. Truitt

No. Cr. 07-16-79 Defendant

GRAND JURY INDICTMENT

THE GRAND JURY CHARGES:

The Grand Jury of the county of Loudoun upon their oath or affirmation do present that CARL L. TRUITT on or about the 17th day of April, 2016 in the county of Loudoun in the Commonwealth of Virginia willfully, deliberately and with premeditation did murder CANDICE C. CAVANAUGH, in violation of the Virginia Criminal Code §18.2.32.

I hereby certify that the foregoing indictment is a true bill.
APPROVED:

    David Frank
    /s/ David Frank
    Foreperson   July 20, 2016

Virginia Criminal Code §18.2-32.

First and second degree murder defined; punishment:

Murder…by…any willful, deliberate, and premeditated killing…is murder of the first degree, punishable as a Class 2 felony.

All murder other than capital murder and murder in the first degree is murder of the second degree and is punishable by confinement in a state correctional facility for not less than five nor more than forty years.

                              * * *

The defendant, Carl Truitt, is on trial, indicted for the murder of his business partner, Candice "Candy" Cavanaugh. Truitt and Cavanaugh operated a small, but attractive restaurant with a diverse menu, well-prepared dishes, a friendly wait staff and an excellent, if limited, wine cellar. But Cavanaugh had a gambling problem and had incurred significant losses over the last six months.

Addicted, she "knew" her luck would change. To feed her addiction, she contacted a small-time local hoodlum, Ray Gotti, (who had changed his last name in emulation of his hero, John Gotti, "The Don") to borrow the funds needed to continue her gambling. On the few occasions she did win, she would pay Gotti what he had advanced, plus interest at twenty-five percent. But after a few days passed she would ask for another loan.

As the cliché goes, you can't beat the "House." Soon, Candy was deep in debt again. After she missed three payments, Gotti refused to advance any more money and started applying the pressure.

Having no other sources of funds, Candy started embezzling from her partnership with Truitt. But with her losses mounting, exacerbated by the interest, Cavanaugh's debt to Gotti had reached over $250,000. Worse, her embezzlements had exhausted the partnership's cash as Gotti continued to warn her several times to "pay up or else."

Cavanaugh could cover up her embezzlement because she was the partner in charge of financial matters. Truitt managed the restaurant. But Truitt finally noticed that something was wrong when the partnership's suppliers started to delay or refuse to fulfill orders unless they were paid in advance. Truitt then hired an accountant to determine the financial condition of the partnership. As a result, he learned Cavanaugh had been siphoning off the partnership's funds to the point of its being bankrupt. The morning after learning of Cavanaugh's betrayal, Truitt called her into his office when she showed up for work. Enraged, he started yelling and cursing. Some of the staff, who could not help but overhear Truitt's rampage, recall him threatening to kill Cavanaugh. Some days later, Candy's nude body was found in the freezer compartment of the restaurant.

Detective Keith Thornton, having worked many cases involving organized crime, decides the crime scene indicated Cavanaugh was the victim of a mob hit. When he learned that Cavanaugh was in debt to Gotti, he became the chief suspect in her murder. On further investigation, Thornton learns that Cavanaugh was embezzling from the partnership to pay off Gotti's loans which had bankrupted the partnership. He also learns that when Truitt found out about Cavanaugh's taking partnership funds, he became enraged and threatened to kill her. When he then finds out that under a Buy-Sell Agreement, Truitt, as the surviving partner, would receive an insurance payment of a half- million dollars in the event of Cavanaugh's death, he drops the charges against Gotti and arrests Truitt for Cavanaugh's murder.

Because Cavanaugh died in a freezer from hyperthermia, the autopsy report fails to establish a time of death. But the victim's DNA found at the scene turned up evidence of intoxication and sexual activity which might explain why she was found naked. Yet, a search of the restaurant did not find any of her clothes.

Truitt's fingerprints were found on the freezer door and handle and throughout the restaurant. The police did not find any of Gotti's fingerprints at the crime scene or the surrounding areas of the restaurant.

Truitt was put on trial for the murder of Candice Cavanaugh.

Readers: The chapters in this book are written as a transcript of the trial. The author's intent is that you will be able to "hear" and evaluate the testimony of witnesses for the prosecution and the defense, the arguments of the prosecuting attorney and defense counsel. You are given the court's jury instructions and then you will read about the deliberations of the jurors after the case is handed to them to reach a verdict. That final chapter is written in more standard novelistic format.

But, this book does not provide a verdict. Each reader must reach his or her own verdict of whether Carl Truitt is guilty or innocent of the charge of first-degree murder of Candice Cavanaugh.

CHAPTER 1

"Hear Ye, Hear Ye"

"All rise. The Court will come to order. Judge Matthew J. Walters, presiding."

"Please be seated, ladies and gentlemen.

"This is a criminal prosecution of the defendant, Carl Truitt. The defendant is accused of murder in the first degree in the death of Candice Cavanaugh. Mr. Truitt has pleaded not guilty. Counsel, may I have your appearances?"

"Yes, Your Honor. Audrey Payne, Office of the Commonwealth Attorney."

"Thank you. And for the defense?"

"Janet Lyle for the defense, Your Honor."

"Thank you. Are counsels ready to proceed?"

"For the Commonwealth, yes, Your Honor."

"The defense is ready."

"Are there any preliminary matters to attend to?"

"Not for the prosecution, Your Honor."

"None for the defense, Your Honor."

"Will counsel be making opening statements?"

"For the prosecution, yes, Your Honor."

"The defense will make a brief opening statement, Your Honor."

"Very well. Ms. Payne, you may proceed."

"Thank you, Your Honor. Ladies and Gentlemen of the jury, the Commonwealth will present testimony and evidence that will show that the defendant, Mr. Truitt, did willfully and with pre-meditation murder his former partner, Candice Cavanaugh. His motive? Anger, revenge, and financial salvation. You will hear testimony that the defendant learned that his partner Cavanaugh had embezzled hundreds of thousands of dollars from the partnership, forcing it into bankruptcy.

"You will hear testimony that the defendant confronted Ms. Cavanaugh in his office the day after he learned of the embezzlement. He became enraged and threatened to kill her. The prosecution will present evidence that the defendant not only had a motive, but also the means and the opportunity to do so. These three elements of a crime are supported by the investigation of the crime scene by a twenty-year veteran of the County's homicide squad. The eyewitness testimony of one who saw the defendant and the victim arguing in the restaurant's hallway near the freezer where the victim's body was later discovered.

"Ladies and gentlemen, this is as close to an open- and-shut case as there is. Motive! Opportunity! Means! Mr. Truitt had all three. After completion of the trial, you will bring in a verdict of guilty as charged. Thank you for your attention."

"Ms. Lyle, please proceed."

"Thank you, Your Honor. Ladies and gentlemen, as you all may know, the prosecution's burden of proof requires that its evidence and testimony must prove to you that Mr. Truitt is guilty beyond a reasonable doubt. The defense will call three witnesses. Mr. Truitt will testify in his own defense. The second witness to be called by the defense has a criminal record. His testimony will be attacked by the prosecution as not credible because of his record. But, listen to his testimony carefully. Don't prejudge it.

"Indeed, the prosecution itself is relying on the testimony of a witness with an even longer rap sheet, Ray Gotti. Again, don't prejudge. Listen closely to Mr. Gotti's testimony, but keep it in context. By that I mean, consider Mr. Gotti's testimony after you have heard the testimony of Mr. Brian Grant, a criminologist and private investigator who will testify for the defense. When all the testimony and evidence is submitted, we are confident that the prosecution has not and cannot show beyond a reasonable doubt that Mr. Truitt is guilty of murdering Ms. Cavanaugh. Thank you."

CHAPTER 2

Autopsy

"Ms. Payne, call your first witness."

"Yes, Your Honor. The Commonwealth calls Dr. Dennis Huber."

"Please raise your right hand. Do you swear to tell the truth, the whole truth, and nothing but the truth?

"Yes."

"Please be seated."

"Dr. Huber, please tell us your background and why you are appearing here today."

"I'm the County Medical Examiner. I'm a pathologist by education and training. My job is to conduct autopsies to determine the cause of death of victims of crime or of death caused by circumstances other than natural causes that may have relevance to public concerns. I am appearing here today to testify on my findings in connection with the death of Ms. Candice Cavanaugh and the circumstances surrounding her death."

"Thank you. How soon after Ms. Cavanaugh's body was found did you arrive on the scene to conduct your initial analysis?"

"I would say less than an hour."

"What did you find?"

"I found Ms. Cavanaugh's body."

"In what condition?"

"Her body was still frozen."

"Still frozen? Is that important?"

"Yes."

"Please explain."

"To do an effective autopsy on a frozen body, it has to be defrosted slowly. If not, the outer body will decompose, but the inner organs will remain frozen and some possibly important evidence could be lost."

"So, how did you handle your examination?"

"Well, first I looked over the scene carefully for anything that might affect my autopsy."

"What would you have been looking for?"

"I would look at the position of the body. Whether there were any marks, cuts on the body, other evidence of a possible cause of death other than or in addition to freezing. I would examine what the victim was wearing. But in this case the body was unclothed, nude."

"Did you find anything at the scene that might be relevant to your autopsy?"

"I did notice she was lying in a fetal position. Her knees brought up to her chest and her head bent down toward her chest. This would be normal for someone trying to stay as warm as possible. I also noticed some marks or bruises on her body. But a quick analysis did not indicate they were possible causes of death."

"Does this complete your account of your inspection at the scene of the crime?"

"Yes."

"What did you do next?"

"Her body was placed in a body bag and taken to the County morgue where I would conduct my autopsy."

"When did you begin your autopsy?"

"A week later."

"A week later? Why so long?"

"As I explained, to conduct an autopsy of a frozen body, it must first thaw. To thaw properly it must be kept in a refrigeration unit at a steady 38 degrees Fahrenheit. As such, it takes a week to thaw out. But properly thawing out the corpse is necessary.

"What were your findings?"

"First, freezing to death takes time. Normal core body temperature, as most know, is 98.6 degrees Fahrenheit. Hypothermia sets in at about 95 degrees. Then there's a progression. At 91 degrees, the person can experience amnesia. This would affect the person's ability to look for means of escape, even if there were few or none. At 82 degrees, the person loses consciousness and that's the beginning of the end, of course. When the temperature falls below 70 degrees, death usually occurs."

"Usually occurs, Doctor?"

"Well, people have been known to survive at lower temperatures. The last I looked, the lowest body temperature of a person that survived was 56.7 degrees. But that was likely due to particular circumstances. Although the person was submerged in icy water for a length of time, he was pulled out and treated in time. So, he survived. Here, the victim was shut off from any help.

"Did your autopsy establish a time of death?"

"Establishing time of death caused by freezing is very difficult. Usually, impossible. At times, educated guesses can be made. But the actual time can be hours off. Instead, I tried to determine how long it took for her to succumb. Commercial freezers are maintained at zero to ten degrees Fahrenheit. The time it takes for anyone to freeze to death will depend on clothing, and the amount and distribution of body fat. A fat or obese person will last longer than a thin person because they have—like a whale—more blubber surrounding their internal organs to keep them warm.

"In the victim's case, she had no clothing. I'll get back to this fact.

"The first sign of freezing is frostbite. This means your tissues are being frozen. Frostbite causes a loss of feeling and a white or pale appearance in extremities, such as fingers, toes, ear lobes, or the tip of the nose. Then the heart pumps less blood to the brain, depriving it of oxygen and causing hallucinations. The heart and respiratory system slow down. Enzymes in the brain are less efficient, causing mental fog, confusion, and disorientation.

"Then there's a strange phenomenon, called paradoxical undressing. We are not exactly sure why this happens. But the accepted theory is that the blood vessels near the surface of the skin suddenly dilate because the muscles that have been constricting them are exhausted. The sudden dilation of the vessels causes one to feel extremely hot all of a sudden. The paradoxical undressing occurs right before one loses consciousness. Finally, the heart rate and breathing rate are so slow that staying awake is impossible. One might consider this a blessing. Once asleep, the suffering stops."

"You said you'd return to the undressing factor?"

"Yes. If the victim was clothed when she went into the freezer, we would have found her clothing she would have discarded as a result of the paradoxical undressing phenomenon. Since we didn't find any, she must have gone or been forced into the freezer without any clothing."

"Is there a particular significance you attach to this fact, Doctor?"

"Yes. Once the body was thawed, we found evidence of recent sexual activity and that she had been drinking. That would be consistent."

"Consistent? I'm not following, Doctor."

"The suppositions are that she was drinking, possibly drunk, and naked because of sexual activity prior to her being put into or entering the freezer."

"Were you able to obtain any DNA due to this activity?"

"Other than hers? No."

"Is that unusual?"

"Yes and no. If the activity involved another person as is usually the case, then his or her DNA would be found. If the activity was solo, that would explain why there wasn't someone else's DNA found."

"Any other possibilities?"

"If there was another person and he or she used protection, it's possible that was the reason we didn't find any other DNA."

"Can you bring together your findings, doctor?"

"On time of death, as I've said, what we could use is not very accurate. But, in this case, she had to go into, or was forced into, the freezer when the restaurant was closed. Due to the lack of funds, the restaurant had been closed for several days before her body was discovered."

"Who discovered the body?"

"A staff member. My understanding is that it was decided to take an inventory of the restaurant's supplies, equipment, and food stuffs. The latter would of course include the food, meats, fish, and so forth in the freezer. During the course of doing that, the freezer was opened and the body was found as I have described it."

"Our investigation indicated that the first staff member arrived just before ten a.m. on April 23rd and he said he entered the freezer around eleven a.m. So, when would you say she died, Doctor?"

"As I have said, there are many factors involved in how long it takes for a person to freeze to death. Given she had a slender body and no clothes on, she could have succumbed in a matter of hours; three or four, maybe a bit more. But that doesn't tell us whether she froze to death on the 23rd or some number of days before then. What we do know, however, is that it had to be sometime between

April 17th and the 23rd."

"Why is that, Doctor?"

"There are records. Written transactions made by the victim. The latest that were found were dated April 17th. Based on these, her death would have occurred between April 18th and the day her body was found on the 23rd."

"Let me ask you this, Doctor. Does time of death in this case have the same relevance as in other cases?"

"If I understand your point, I would say no."

"Why?"

"She was effectively murdered when she was forced into the freezer. The time she actually succumbed doesn't provide the usual clues as to who may have been responsible."

"Can you amplify on that?"

"Let's say someone is shot to death. We arrive at the scene and establish the time of death based on the fact that the victim died instantly from the gun shot. The police investigation would then focus on suspects that do not have an alibi based on proof they were somewhere else at or around the time of the shooting. The time of death. In this case, any suspects would base their alibi on proof they were somewhere else on the nights of April 18th to the 23rd. These dates are the closest we can come to the time she was forced into the freezer."

"Anything else, Doctor?"

"Well, the body was found at eleven a.m. on the 23rd. Since a body can freeze in four hours, we can surmise that the time period when she was forced into the freezer was as far back as April 18th to as recently as the night of April 22nd or the morning of April 23rd."

"Thank you, Doctor. That is all."

"Any questions, Ms. Lyle?"

"A few, Your Honor. Thank you."

"As you know, Doctor, I am defense counsel for the defendant, Mr. Carl Truitt."

"Yes, I know."

"And you know, Mr. Truitt was Ms. Cavanaugh's partner?"

"Yes."

"And it is customary, even required, that in a murder case, the entire premises—or at least the portions of the premises that are near the scene of the crime—are dusted for fingerprints and DNA?"

"Yes."

"And therefore, these procedures were followed in this case?"

"Yes."

"What areas of the restaurant were covered by the search for prints and DNA?"

"The freezer, of course. The hallway leading to the freezer that also extended to the back door of the restaurant, the back door, the victim's office, Mr. Truitt's office, and the office I understand was used by the accountant Mr. Truitt hired."

"What were the results?"

"You'd have to ask the police about the fingerprints."

"And the DNA samples?"

"DNA samples were collected from the places I just mentioned."

"Whose DNA did you find and where?"

We found the victim's DNA samples in her office and in Mr. Truitt's. We found Mr. Truitt's DNA in his office and the victim's office."

"On what did you find Mr. Truitt's DNA in Ms. Cavanaugh's office?"

"It was on a coffee cup."

"Did you find anyone else's DNA on this cup?"

"Yes. It was that of Mr. Truitt's secretary."

"What about Ms. Cavanaugh's clothes?"

"My understanding is that despite a thorough search, her clothes have not been found."

"I see. Thank you, Doctor. That's all."

CHAPTER 3

Witness For The Prosecution

Paul Engel

The Commonwealth calls Mr. Paul Engel."

"Do you swear to tell the truth, the whole truth, and nothing but the truth?"

"Yes."

"Please state your full name."

"My name is Paul R. Engel."

"What is your occupation, Mr. Engel?"

"I am a certified public accountant in private practice."

"Are your clients individuals, businesses, or other organizations?"

"My clientele includes all of those."

"Businesses, like the Buon Appetito Restaurant, owned by the defendant and Ms. Cavanaugh?"

"Yes."

"Is the Buon Appetito one of your clients?"

"Not a regular client, no."

"Not a regular client? What does that mean?"

"I was hired by Mr. Truitt as a forensic accountant. Before I was asked to investigate the finances and accounting records of his and Ms. Cavanaugh's partnership, I hadn't done any work for him or the partnership."

"Let me show you this document. Please review while I

provide copies to the court and defense counsel."

PAUL ENGEL
Cpa, Forensic Accounting

Education
University of Virginia
B.S. Accounting 1996

Profession
Certified Public Accountant (CPA) 1996 to present

Licensure
Virginia Board of Accountancy

Employment
Coopers & Lybrand 1996 to 1998
PriceWaterHouseCoopers 1998 to 2006 (Price Waterhouse and Coopers merged in 1998)
The Firm of Paul Engel, Certified Public Accountant, 2006 to present

Memberships
American Institute of Certified Public Accountants (AICPA)
Virginia Society of CPAs (VSCPA)
National Association of Forensic Accountants (NAFA)

Professional Accomplishments and Continuing Professional Certifications
Scored 98% on AICPA's Professional Ethics: AICPA's Comprehensive Course (A score of 90% required for VASCPA license)
Annual Certificates of Completion of 40 hours of Continuing Professional Education
Certificate of Completion of Virginia-Specific Ethics Course 2016 (Annual Requirement)
NAFA Certifications 2006-present

"Do you recognize it?"

"Yes."

"What is it?"

"It's a true and accurate copy of my curriculum vitae."

"Please mark this as Exhibit 1 for the prosecution. You don't need to read all of it, but can you highlight a few of the entries that describe your professional background?"

"Yes. I graduated from the University of Virginia in 1981 with a Bachelor of Science degree cum laude in accounting. I received an award as the top student of all the graduates in accounting in that year. After graduation, I went to work for one of what was then called the 'Big Eight' accounting firms as an auditor. Within three years, I was promoted to manager.

"Two years later, I opened my own accounting firm, the Firm of Paul Engel, Certified Public Accountant. Today, the firm has four partners, one being myself, of course. The firm provides full-service accounting expertise. In addition to audit work, preparation of financial statements, various accounting analyses, I specialize in forensic accounting. Forensic accountants are like medical examiners. Medical examiners look for causes of a person's death. We look for accounting irregularities, use of improper or erroneous accounting methods and practices, and advise management with the most accurate financial information about the business.

"The objective of forensic accounting engagement is to provide an accounting specific to the issue or issues as presented by the client. Unlike other audits and attestations, the forensic accountant is responsible only to the client as opposed, for example, to shareholders or regulatory authorities. Ultimately, the objective is to reach conclusions that remove any debate over what the financial records disclose. When forensic accounting is used in fraud investigations, it is conducted after the fact. A special mission for a forensic accountant is to look for possible fraud. Here, the purpose is to reduce the incidence of fraud and white-collar crime and to assist the client in detection and deterrence."

"You indicated you were specifically hired by the defendant as a forensic accountant. Is that right?"

"Yes. Carl Truitt contacted me on the day after I had made a presentation to the local Chamber of Commerce on several different business and financial practices, including the controls needed to detect, deter, and prevent employee embezzlement."

"Did Mr. Truitt mention he was concerned about possible fraud when he first contacted you?"

"No. He called me and asked if I would run an audit of the partnership's books and records. He did express concern about the financial condition of his business. He simply wanted to know why his restaurant, the Buon Appetito, was in the red even though bookings were solid, with a good percentage of repeat customers."

"Did Mr. Truitt mention anything about his partner, Ms. Cavanaugh, at the time?

"Yes. He explained that Ms. Cavanaugh was his partner."

"Did he mention any suspicion or concern about Ms. Cavanaugh at the time?"

"No. He did not at the time mention anything about a suspicion of fraud or wrongdoing by anybody."

"What did you do after Mr. Truitt retained your services?"

"I began some preliminary due diligence. I learned that the restaurant had been in operation for just over three years. With that in mind, I did some research on the restaurant business and discovered a study that showed that the highest failure rate in the restaurant industry was during the first year. Over a quarter of restaurants fail. About another twenty percent fail in the second year and ten percent more in the third year. Well over half of new restaurants, therefore, fail in the first three years. That struck me as a bit odd for Buon Appetito. Because as part of my research, I discovered it enjoyed a good reputation among diners and had received positive reviews from a number of critics."

"When did you start your actual investigation?"

"I toured the restaurant facilities the following day. I wanted to get a feel for the day-to-day management, and an overview of the company's financial records and record keeping. I also told Mr. Truitt that for a complete financial review, audit, and forensic investigation, I would need complete access to all accounting records for a period of two weeks starting the following week. I advised him that I would need to work on site to have access to all of the records but assured him that he could continue business as usual. I quoted him a flat fee of $15,000. And because I knew that the restaurant was on shaky ground, I demanded to receive my fees in advance. Mr. Truitt agreed to the arrangement and paid me out of his personal funds."

"Once you started your investigation, what did you learn at first?"

"When I arrived the first day at the restaurant, I went into Mr. Truitt's office to discuss arrangements. During this discussion, I learned that he was not involved with any aspects of the accounting for the business. Mr. Truitt's talents and work focused on creativity with food preparation, restaurant style, and service. Ms. Cavanaugh was the partner who handled the financial matters of the business."

"Did you meet with Ms. Cavanaugh at this time?"

"No. She was not in the restaurant."

"Do you know when she learned of your investigation?"

"No. I don't know when she was told about my working there. So, I don't know what, if any, reaction she may have had when first told."

"Was she present when you were working at the restaurant?"

"Yes. She was there from time to time over the course of the week I worked there."

"Did she inquire who you were and what you were doing?"

"She never asked directly, but I'm sure she knew. I'm sure Mr. Truitt told her at some point."

"Did she show any signs of curiosity?"

"No."

"Interest?"

"No."

"Did she seem concerned?"

"If she did, she didn't show any signs."

"Did she seem suspicious or act suspicious?"

"I didn't notice anything particularly suspicious about her actions or demeanor in general while I was going through the books and records during the two weeks I was there."

"You say in general. What do you mean?"

"There were two times when Ms. Cavanaugh was in the office where I was working. I had some cancelled checks, bank statements, and ledger cards on the desk. She spilled coffee all over the records. At first, I thought it was an accident. When she did it a second time, I thought she was clumsy. But thinking about it after the fact, I concluded maybe the spills were intentional. That she was trying to destroy the records."

"Were these records destroyed?"

"Not all, but some. However, there were many other records. So, if her intent was to destroy these, it didn't do her much good."

"Are these the only two incidents you recall about her during your time at the restaurant?"

"I did overhear a few conversations that she had on the phone.

One was the first week I was there. Then two or three times the following week. I heard her tell the person on the phone, 'I promised you I would get the money, just give me time.' Then I heard, 'There's no need to use threats, you'll get your money.' Then again, 'Yes, I remember what happened last time when the payment wasn't timely. Please don't. That won't be necessary. I'll pay you, I promise.' She was upset by the calls, but didn't seem scared. Initially, I thought her conversations were with a vendor."

"Why was that?"

"In the restaurant business, if you can't pay your bills, the deliveries stop, and the business goes belly up. In retrospect, I think these telephone conversations were probably between Ms. Cavanaugh and Ray Gotti."

"Ray Gotti? How do you know Mr. Gotti?"

"During the two weeks I was at the restaurant, I frequently saw a person in the shadows in the alley across the street from the restaurant's back door. At the time, I just assumed he worked at the business across the street and was taking a cigarette break. But after seeing this person several times, I finally recalled seeing his picture in the papers and recognized him."

"You recognized Mr. Gotti. But why connect him to Ms. Cavanaugh's phone calls you overheard?"

"At first, I didn't. But after I recognized him and recalled the newspaper accounts of his run-ins with the law, it made sense. That is, what she said took on a new meaning for me. Her statements were pleading for time, promising to pay, saying there was no need for making threats."

"But you don't know it was Gotti she was talking to."

"No. I never heard who was on the other side of the conversation or what the caller said. Ms. Cavanaugh never spoke about it with me. And I didn't ask her. But, there's this. During the first week I was there, Ms. Cavanaugh came into the restaurant and had a burn mark on her hand. And another time, she had bruising on her neck. Like someone had grabbed her neck hard. I didn't ask her any questions though."

"Let's return to your investigation of the accounting records. What other findings or conclusions did you have?"

"Well, let me start by saying that restaurants are notorious for losing money due to employee embezzlement. The most common scheme is known as 'skimming.' Skimming siphons off cash receipts that are pocketed by the employee, or in this case, one of the owners. These are not recorded in the accounting system. Retail establishments and particularly restaurants are vulnerable to this type of scheme when the customers pay in cash.

"A related type of scheme is to ring up a sale for less than the actual amount. The cashier simply pockets the difference between the actual sale amount and the amount input to the computer record. An employee, manager, or owner may also record the actual amount of the customer's check and then void that entry, allowing him or her to pocket the cash paid by the customer."

"Are there others?"

"Yes. If an employee collects the cash and makes the bank deposit, he or she has an excellent opportunity to misappropriate company funds. The employee receives the daily receipts from the cashier, along with the cash register tapes. The employee then mutilates the register tapes so they can't be read. With the tapes destroyed, the employee pockets a portion of the day's receipts and deposits the balance. Unless the daily deposit amounts are compared with the cash register tapes, the fraud goes undetected."

"Did you find evidence of these schemes in the records for Buon Appetito?" Payne asked.

"Yes. But I kept in mind that most payments for meals today

are paid by credit card. What I found is that only a small percentage of Buon Appetito's customers paid cash."

"So, what did that tell you, if anything?"

"First, it told me that the methods I just described would have provided only part of the amount of cash that would have bankrupted the company. Second, it told me that I had to consider what other means were used to siphon off the company's funds."

"What did you consider?"

"Checks are often instruments of fraud. Employees with signature authority, and of course, managers and owners, can make checks payable to cash or to themselves personally. The person with check signatory authority simply writes the check to himself or herself or to cash. Then he or she marks the check as being void in the company's check register and then inflates the amount of another check written, for example, to a company supplier. When the bank statements are received, the checks are removed and destroyed.

"But in this case, I focused on 'check kiting.' It's a form of check fraud that involves taking advantage of the float to make use of non-existent funds in a checking or other bank account.

"Most commonly this involves writing a check for a value greater than the account balance from an account in one bank, then writing a check from another account in another bank, also with non-sufficient funds, with the second check serving to cover the non-existent funds from the first account. The purpose of check kiting is to falsely inflate the balance of a checking account in order to allow written checks to clear that would otherwise bounce.

"But what caught my attention was the form of check fraud that involves the use of a second bank or a third party, often a place of retail. This is done in order to delay the absence of funds in a <u>transactional account</u> on the day the check is due to clear at the bank. Such acts are frequently committed by bankrupt or temporarily unemployed individuals or small businesses seeking emergency loans. It is also used by start-up businesses or other struggling businesses seeking interest-free financing while intending to make good on their balances. But most relevant to this case is the fact that this method is used by pathological gamblers who have the expectation of depositing funds upon winning."

"So, if you conclude that Ms. Cavanaugh used this method, on what would your conclusion be based?"

"In performing my forensic investigation, I reviewed the following financial and business records. General ledger, journal entries, adjusted journal entries, trial balances, checking accounts, cancelled checks, deposit slips, cash register receipts, order tickets, and vendor invoices. I also personally interviewed both Mr. Truitt and Ms. Cavanaugh, as well as a couple of the restaurant employees to understand the flow of money, and internal controls present in the company. Although both Truitt and Cavanaugh had authority to sign checks, Cavanaugh primarily assumed that role. Truitt managed the kitchen staff, the menus, ordered food supplies, scheduled employees, reservations, and kept the customers happy. Cavanaugh oversaw the processing of customer payments during and after business hours and managed the financial aspects of the business.

"During the first week of my investigation, I started to suspect that Cavanaugh had been stealing from the restaurant. I didn't mention my suspicions to anyone. But after I had completed my two-week forensic investigation, it was evident that Cavanaugh had been misappropriating funds from Buon Appetitto for some time. I found evidence of each of the typical embezzlement schemes mentioned previously. For example, skimming had occurred. There were several instances where one of the waiters or waitresses had a carbon copy of an order ticket in their book. But the order was not included in the cash register receipt for that day."

"Excuse me, Mr. Engel, let me show you this document. Do you recognize it?"

Buon Appetito
April 10, 2016

1 Tito's Blood Orange Cosmo	$6.00
1 Italian Margarita	$5.00
1 Insalata della casa	$7.50
1 Insalata caprese	$9.00
1 Banfi Chianti Classico	$30.00
1 Trota di fiume	$22.00
1 Piccata di vitello	$20.00
1 Tenderloin medallions	$26.00
1 Pescatore almafi	$25.00
1 Grilled asparagus	$ 2.50
1 Sautéed spinach w/lemon butter	$ 2.50
Subtotal	$155.50
Tax	9.33
Total	$164.83

"Yes, I do."

"Please tell the court and members of the jury what it is."

"It is a carbon copy of an order ticket in one of the waiter's or waitress' order books, but this order was not included in the cash register receipts for the day it was made."

"I see. Thank you. Please mark this as Commonwealth Exhibit 2."

"Reviewing this order ticket, what can you tell us about it?"

"I cross-checked the order tickets to the daily cash register receipts. I cannot say for certain that the skimming is attributable to Cavanaugh. Someone else could have been managing the cash register at the time. However, in looking at all the events, there are others that directly point to Cavanaugh. For example, certain daily cash register tapes did not match to the deposits that were made. These deposit slips were written in Cavanaugh's handwriting. They were part of her normal job responsibilities, and not the responsibility of any other employee."

"You're not a handwriting expert are you, Mr. Engel?"

"No."

"Then how can you say that it is Ms. Cavanaugh's handwriting on this order ticket?"

"I reviewed many documents signed by Ms. Cavanaugh and her handwriting is the same on all such documents. And as I said, handling the deposits was part of Ms. Cavanaugh's responsibilities."

"Let me show you this document. Do you recognize it?"

Buon Appetito Acct# 0000155178637

Deposit - April 10, 2016

Coins -	25.57
Cash -	437.00
Checks -	375.47
Subtotal -	838.04
Less cash rec'd -	----
Total -	838.04

Community Banks of Virginia, Leesburg, VA.

"Yes."

"Please tell us what it is."

"It is a Buon Appetito deposit slip in the amount for $838.04 for Tuesday April 19, 2016."

"We will mark this as Commonwealth Exhibit 3 and submit for the record. Do you recognize these two documents?"

Cash Register Receipts April 16, 2016	Cash Register Receipts April 17, 2016
243.96√	196.53√
119.43√	102.43√
78.55√	89.14√
87.87√	145.15√
146.44√	167.76√
175.05√	94.56√
84.25√	88.88√
99.93√	101.22√
143.16√	245.57√
156.14√	176.06√
146.23√	248.84√
64.64√	56.60√
156.00√	91.11√
256.42√	187.77√
85.40√	126.43√
99.17√	200.15√
84.54√	132.32√
87.59√	158.80√
76.69√	234.46√
155.85√	232.65√
2,843.78√	2,162.69√

"Yes, this one is Buon Appetito's cash register tape for Saturday, April 16 and this one is the tape for Sunday, April 17."

"We will mark these Commonwealth Exhibits 4 and 5 and submit them for the record. What do these cash register tapes show?"

"The register tape for Saturday the 16th shows receipts from Friday in the amount of $2,162.69. The tape for Sunday the 17th, Exhibit 5, shows receipts for $2,843.78. A total of $5,006.47.

"That's a $4,168.43 difference between the deposit slip for $838.04 and these cash register tapes for $5006.47. That's a significant difference of course. But it's a small amount in the overall scheme of things."

"Can you explain your last statement?"

"Yes. I found much larger amounts in the checks that were written to cash or to Ms. Cavanaugh herself. While these were shown as void in the check register, these and other checks actually cleared the bank."

"Let me show you this document and ask if you recognize it."

```
BUON APPETITO                                    4859
                                               68-624/415
14995 High Street
Leesburg, VA 20175                             4/18/16
                                                 Date

Pay to the order of:  Candice Cavanaugh        $ 4,500
   Four Thousand Five Hundred & 00/100
                                                Dollars
Community Bank of Virginia       -Classic-       BANKING

For  Draw                             C. Cavanaugh

|:041540 620|:000155178637| |:04859
```

"Yes, I do."

"What is it?"

"It's a check drawn on Buon Appetito's bank account."

"Let me show you this document and ask if you recognize it."

"Yes, I do. It's a page from Buon Appetito's check register recording checks written and deposits made for the period from April 12, 2016 through April 16, 2016."

"We'll submit as Commonwealth's Exhibit 6."

BUON APPETITTO REGISTER

			$25,689.25
4/12/16	4854 Loudoun Farms	1,700.00	23,989.25
4/12/16	4855 Superior Meats	2,500.00	21,489.25
4/13/16	4856 Virginia Vintners	3,000.00	18,489.25
4/13/16	deposit	850.00	19,339.25
4/14/16	4857 NOVA Supplies	1,200.00	18,139.25
4/14/16	deposit	2,000.00	20,139.25
4/15/16	4858 Restaurant Linens	500.00	19,639.25
4/15/16	4859 ~~C. Cavanaugh~~ VOID		
4/16/16	4860 Old Dominion Electric	340.00	19,299.25

"And looking at the page opened in the register, what do you see?"

"I see a listing of a check made out to Ms. Cavanaugh with a line striking over it and the word 'void' next to it."

"What else can you tell from these entries?"

"I saw similar entries made out to cash or Candice Cavanaugh that were crossed out and the word 'void' following the entry. Each time they were on amounts recorded. To balance the account, another check in the check register and ledger account was manipulated to increase the payments to cover the amounts of the 'voided' checks to cash and to Candice Cavanaugh."

"Did you find other occurrences of this manipulation?"

"Yes. In total, I uncovered 167 instances of embezzlement committed by Ms. Cavanaugh totaling $389,285 over the past two years. It appears that no embezzlement occurred during the first year that the restaurant was in operation. Of the 167 instances of embezzlement, more than half occurred in the six-month period prior to February 2016. These embezzlements left the business operating at a net loss of $216,445 with a negative cash flow. In addition, I found records that show that vendors have refused to supply product to the restaurant until outstanding accounts payable were brought current."

"What did you do after learning of the embezzlement?

"I told Mr. Truitt. This was on Friday, February 19, 2016 about 4:00 p.m. I informed him that my forensic investigation revealed that Buon Appetito was bankrupt due to the embezzlement by his partner, Candice Cavanaugh, and that the amount embezzled was $389,285.

At first, Truitt appeared to be in shock, repeating several times, 'How could this happen?' The more I detailed the instances of the embezzlement and cited examples of the skimming, check fraud, and deposit manipulation, he got red in the face, started pacing back and forth, smashing his fist into his other hand. At one point, he stopped pacing and looked at me."

"What did he do then?"

"He said, 'Well, I'll make Cavanaugh pay for this. She won't make a fool out of me.'"

"Then what happened?"

"He told me that I had done my job. That I should leave and

he would confront Cavanaugh by himself."

"Did you leave at that point?"

"Yes. But after I left, I realized that I had left some of my notes on the desk in the office I was working in. When I went back to retrieve them, I saw Mr. Truitt talking to Ms. Cavanaugh."

"Did you overhear what was being said?"

"I couldn't hear everything that was said. But, I heard Ms. Cavanaugh say something about gambling and then Truitt yelled that she had to come up with the money right now and was shaking his fist at her. And then I did hear Truitt say, 'You'll pay for this! Big time!' Then I left."

"What did you think when you heard this?"

"Well, I thought, she has no money. He must have something else in mind."

"You mean something else to make her pay since she had no money to pay with?"

"Yes."

"I will show you this document and ask if you have seen it before."

BUY-SELL AGREEMENT

This agreement is made this 5th day of June, 2012 by and between Carl Truitt (Truitt) and Candice Cavanaugh (Cavanaugh).

WHEREAS, Truitt and Cavanaugh are equal partners in T&C Partnership d/b/a Buon Appetito (Partnership); and

WHEREAS, to ensure the continuity of management

in and ownership of the Partnership;

NOW THEREFORE, it is hereby agreed as follows:

1. In the event of the death of a partner, by natural causes, illness, accident, acts of God or the independent acts of third parties, the surviving partner shall purchase from the estate of the deceased partner, his or her interest in the Partnership.

2. Until otherwise agreed to, each partnership interest represents fifty percent (50%) of the value of the Partnership. For purposes of this Agreement, each Partner's interest in the Partnership is Fifty Thousand Dollars US ($50,000.00). At the end of each calendar year, the Partners shall agree upon the value of their respective shares; provided, however, that if no agreement is reached, the Partners shall retain a financial expert to make an evaluation.

3. To ensure funding to make the purchase, the partners have purchased an insurance policy in the amount of Five Hundred Thousand Dollars US ($500,000.00) on the life of each, naming as beneficiary the surviving partner. The insurance premiums shall be paid as an expense of the Partnership. Additional insurance may be purchased as agreed upon by the Partners.

4. Upon the death of one Partner, the surviving Partner may immediately collect the insurance proceeds of the policy on the life of the deceased Partner and shall pay

the proceeds determined to be due without delay. If the insurance proceeds are not sufficient to purchase the deceased Partner's interest, the surviving Partner shall pay the amount of the deficiency to the deceased Partner's estate; provided, however, that the value of the deceased Partner's interest shall be adjusted to recognize any advances, outstanding debts or liabilities owed to the Partnership by the deceased Partner.

5. If the proceeds of the insurance on the life of the deceased Partner are in excess of the purchase price of the deceased Partner's interest, including adjustments for any advances, debts or liabilities owed the Partnership by the deceased Partner, the surviving Partner shall be entitled to the excess over the purchase price. If for any reason, the purchase price of the deceased Partner's interest is, due to adjustments for advances, debts and liabilities, reduced to zero, the surviving Partner shall be entitled to the entire amount of insurance proceeds.

IN WITNESS, WHEREOF, the Partners have executed this agreement on the date first above written.

<u>Candice Cavanaugh</u>   <u>Carl Truitt</u>

"Yes, I have."

"What is it?"

"While I was reviewing the company records, I came across a Buy-Sell agreement for the restaurant. That's what this document is."

"Please mark this as Commonwealth Exhibit 7. What can you tell us about this Agreement?"

"The Buy-Sell Agreement provides that in the event of the death of one partner, the survivor receives $500,000 from an insurance policy. So, upon Ms. Cavanaugh's death, Mr. Truitt stands to receive $500,000 under the insurance policy."

"In your experience, is such an agreement and payout standard practice?"

"It is not at all unusual for partners in a business to have a Buy-Sell agreement in place funded by insurance. It's a smart business practice. A partner's death can have serious consequences for the business. It loses the talents, experience, and contributions of the partner. If the partner's interest is bequeathed to a family member, there's a risk that someone without the same talents and experience could interfere with running the business. Having an infusion of funds provides options to continue operations on a financially solid basis."

"Thank you, Mr. Engel. That's all the questions I have. Your witness, Ms. Lyle."

* * *

"Mr. Engel, you testified as to your background as an accountant and specifically as a forensic accountant. Have you ever had any complaints about your work?"

"I believe I have an excellent reputation among my peers in both audit work and forensic accounting. All of my peer review examinations have yielded outstanding results. But yes, I was sued for malpractice once. It was several years back."

"What was the result?"

"My malpractice insurance company settled the claim."

"How?"

"It paid a small amount. I don't recall other than that the carrier wanted the matter to just go away. It didn't want the expense of litigating. In any event, the settlement agreement stated that I denied any liability and the case was dismissed."

"You testified you overheard the conversation between Mr. Truitt and Ms. Cavanaugh after it was disclosed that she had bankrupted the company. Correct?"

"Yes."

"Did you hear the whole conversation?"

"No."

"Why was that?"

"The office where I had left my notes was near the kitchen and the staff was preparing for opening. There was a lot of noise made as they got the kitchen and the tables ready for the next seating."

"I see. But you claim you did hear Mr. Truitt threaten Ms. Cavanaugh? Is that correct?

"Yes."

"What happened that made it possible for you to hear that part of the conversation between Mr. Truitt and Ms. Cavanaugh? Did the staff suddenly stop its preparations?"

"I don't recall."

"You said you saw Mr. Truitt's face and described it as being red with anger, correct?"

"Yes."

"What did you suspect would be Mr. Truitt's reaction when you told him about the embezzlement?"

"He'd be mad."

"Did you think he would be mad enough to kill Ms. Cavanaugh?"

"Yes, I suppose I did. As a forensic accountant, I have seen a number of people who have been victimized by such betrayal. They all react angrily."

"Angrily enough to give the impression that they wanted to kill their betrayers?"

"Yes."

"Then is it possible that what you thought you heard as Mr. Truitt's threat to Ms. Cavanaugh was really your conditioned response to your previous experiences?"

"I… I don't know."

"You testified you overheard Ms. Cavanaugh talking to someone over the phone and that she seemed upset. But not afraid. Is that right?"

"Yes."

"You also testified you overheard her say 'you'll get your money; no need for threats.' Is that correct?"

"Yes, or words to that effect."

"You said you didn't know to whom she was talking? But would you disagree that in all likelihood it was Ray Gotti?"

"Objection, Your Honor! Calls for speculation."

"Your Honor, he can testify as to his state of mind at the time. What he was thinking, what his impressions were."

"I agree, Ms. Lyle. Objection overruled. You may answer the question, Mr. Engel, based on your impression of to whom Ms. Cavanaugh was speaking to on the phone at the time."

"Well, at the time I thought she was talking to Mr. Gotti. It just made sense to me that Gotti was threatening Ms. Cavanaugh if she didn't pay her gambling debts."

"Thank you. You testified you saw a figure in the shadows across from the rear entrance to the restaurant. Is that correct?

"Yes."

"And you testified that you finally recognized the person you saw was Mr. Gotti. Is that also correct?"

"Yes."

"What else did you notice about Mr. Gotti's presence at the rear of the restaurant?"

"At first, nothing special."

"At first? Then, did you notice anything later on?"

"Well, after I learned of Ms. Cavanaugh's murder and that she was killed in the restaurant, I thought to myself, if Gotti were in the same position on the night of the murder, he would have a good view of anything going on through the back door to the kitchen and of course just outside it. Despite it being dark at the time, there was a light right above the back door's entrance to the restaurant."

"Would you agree that if Mr. Gotti was in that position on the night of the murder, he would be able to enter the restaurant?"

"Yes. I guess so. I didn't think about that."

"You testified that you heard Mr. Truitt threaten Ms. Cavanaugh? Did you think he was serious? Serious enough to physically harm her? Murder her?"

"I thought he was very, very upset and angry and that he had a right to be."

"Did you tell Ms. Cavanaugh that you overheard Mr. Truitt threaten her?"

"No."

"Did you advise the police about Mr. Truitt's threats to Ms. Cavanaugh?"

"No."

"Did you make any effort to calm Mr. Truitt down?"

"No."

"Did you advise him that you overheard him threaten Ms. Cavanaugh?"

"Why would I do that?"

"To let him know that you knew of the threats so that he might back away from actually attempting to do harm to Ms. Cavanaugh?"

"I didn't think about that."

"You didn't warn Ms. Cavanaugh, or confront Mr. Truitt. Were you indifferent to what might happen because of Mr. Truitt's threats?"

"No."

"Then sitting here today, what were your reasons for not taking any action after hearing Mr. Truitt's threats?"

"Well… I suppose I didn't take them seriously."

"Didn't take what seriously?"

"Mr. Truitt's threats to harm Ms. Cavanaugh."

"Thank you. You are familiar with Buy-Sell agreements of the type that Mr. Truitt and Ms. Cavanaugh had?"

"Yes."

"That agreement was based on an insurance policy. Is that correct?"

"Yes."

"In your experience do insurance policies on someone's life contain a provision that the right to receive the insurance proceeds is forfeit if the death of the insured is caused by the intentional actions of the beneficiary?"

"Yes. That's correct."

"So, if Mr. Truitt did murder Ms. Cavanaugh, he doesn't receive the $500,000 from the insurance, does he?"

"That's correct. He would not receive the insurance proceeds."

"If he is convicted in this trial, you mean?"

"Yes."

"Thank you. I have no further questions."

* * *

"A few questions on redirect, Your Honor."

"Proceed, Ms. Payne."

"To the best of your recollection, did you hear Mr. Truitt threaten Ms. Cavanaugh?"

"Yes."

"Did you think his threat was serious?"

"Yes."

"Then why did you not take some action?"

"After I left the restaurant, I received a call from another client. It was an emergency matter. I had to respond immediately. I didn't even have time to return to the office. I went to the client's office where his business was under a surprise audit by the IRS. I spent the next two days assisting the client. And by that time, I suppose I forgot about Mr. Truitt and Ms. Cavanaugh."

"I see. Thank you."

CHAPTER 4

Witness For The Prosecution

Detective Keith Thornton

"The Commonwealth calls Keith Thornton."

"Please state your name and your occupation."

"My name is Keith Thornton. I am a detective with the Loudoun County Sheriff's Office. I am a twenty-year veteran of law enforcement and hold a Bachelor's degree in Criminal Justice from Virginia Commonwealth University.

During my career, I have been involved in various criminal investigations at the local, state, and federal levels. I served as a member of the Virginia Attorney General's Task Force on Organized Crime. The experience of working in an undercover capacity helped with investigations in which there were indications that organized crime was involved. Using that experience, I have assisted in the successful prosecutions of those connected with organized crime."

"Were you assigned to lead the investigation into the death of Ms. Cavanaugh?"

"Yes."

"Why?"

"I was called in because certain circumstances suggested that organized crime was involved in her death."

"What were those circumstances?"

"Her body was found in the restaurant's freezer. Being 'iced' like that is typical of a mob hit. Then, Mr. Engel identified Ray Gotti outside the restaurant on the night she was murdered. We found out that Cavanaugh owed Gotti hundreds of thousands in loans he made to her that she used to support her gambling habit. The Medical Examiner found cigarette burns on her arm and bruises on other parts of her body that he advised were caused by being struck or beaten.

We also had Mr. Engel's statement that he overheard Ms. Cavanaugh on the phone being threatened and her saying she would pay back some money. And he told us his suspicions that she was talking to Gotti as he testified here today. It doesn't take a genius to figure out that organized crime would be involved in loan sharking to fund a person with a gambling problem. And it's just as well known that those who don't pay up get threatened and roughed up. If the debt is huge and the mobster concludes payback is not likely, resorting to violence is almost certain. A message has to be sent to others who owe the loan sharks money. Based upon these circumstances, we arrested Mr. Gotti on suspicion for the murder of Ms. Cavanaugh."

"Please review the document I'm handing you. Do you recognize it, Detective Thornton?"

CRIME SCENE REPORT #04202014

Date: Saturday 04/23/16

Investigating Officer: Detective Keith Thornton

Type of Inquiry: Homicide

Address/Location:	City/Town	County
14995 High Street,	Leesburg, VA 20175	Loudoun

Apparent cause of death:

Nude body frozen in restaurant freezer

Victim I.D.
Candice Cavanaugh, DOB 1984; Female, 5'6"; 122 lbs.; Blonde hair, blue eyes; burn marks on left arm and hand, bruises on neck, right and left thighs.

Start of investigation:
911 call received. Alerted precinct. Uniform officer dispatched. Arrives at approximately 9:20 a.m, Saturday, 4/23/16. 911 call made by restaurant employee who found body.

Arrived 9:40 a.m. Yellow tape deployed. Spoke with employee who made call. Thomas Ripley. Sous chef. Confirmed no one touched the body or entered the freezer after body found. Autopsy will confirm, but seems obvious the victim died from freezing. Open question! Was she killed and then put into freezer or was she put in the freezer to die?

Access to restaurant included victim, her partner Carl Truitt and a few others – sous chefs, maître de. Working staff needs to be admitted by one of those who have unlimited access. But only Truitt has keys to back door and freezer.

Most of the employees had no idea who would want to harm victim. But sous chef Ripley and maître de, Jefferson Clark, did say they eventually recognized Ray Gotti after he had been to the restaurant several times to visit with the victim in her office. The office doors were always closed. They both said that given the rumors that Cavanaugh had a gambling problem, it made sense and concerned them. They knew she was handling all the revenues, finances, and books for the restaurant.

Monday 04/25/16

11:00 a.m. Interviewed Victim's partner, Carl Truitt. Says he last saw victim Friday, 4/15/16. She was in her office working. It was late. Truitt claims he was unware of her gambling or that she had been embezzling the restaurant's funds. When he discovered the restaurant was losing money, he hired an accountant to find out why. He was shocked when he was told the restaurant was bankrupt and even more shocked when he was told why. He admits to being angry, real angry, and yelled at the victim. He can't remember exactly what he said, but admitted it was threatening. He explained he was unaware the restaurant was in such poor financial condition because he had nothing to do with keeping the books. All accounting and control of funds was in the hands of the victim. His job was running the restaurant, managing staff, preparing offerings, cooking, etc. He did not know who Ray Gotti was. He later was able to identify him from some newspaper stories about him in which a photo of Gotti was included.

This was all before he learned about the victim's embezzlement. When he found out about what was going on and confronted the victim, she showed him her arms which she told him were scarred due to cigarette burns. Showed him bruises on her neck and thighs and that Gotti had threatened to do worse unless she paid up. She told him she owed Gotti six figures, but was unable to be exact. She said she had no other choice than to use the money from the business and that she would pay it back with interest as soon as she started winning again.

11:45 a.m. Gathered the staff together to save time. None knew about the financial state of the restaurant or the reasons for it. When shown a picture of Gotti, several said they saw him several times. He would come in and meet with the victim in her office. On one or more occasions within the time frame in which she could have died, several claim to have seen Gotti in the alley behind the restaurant.

Noon: Searched victim's office. Checked ledgers, check registers, computer. Found routine records pertaining to the business, supplier contracts, accounts receivable, accounts payable. Also found a spreadsheet with dollar entries in a column headed "RG." There were two columns – Debits and Credits. Latest entry was for $308,000 debit.

3:30 p.m: Interviewed Paul Engel at his office. He was hired by Truitt to find out why the restaurant was losing money. His audit lasted two weeks, April 4 thru April 15. He confirmed he found out that the victim had been taking large amounts of money out of the restaurant's earnings. Her most recent take was for $208,000. He was asked how Truitt reacted when he told him what the victim had been up to and that she was the reason the restaurant was bankrupt. He said Truitt was enraged. I asked Engel whether Truitt said or did anything when he was told. Engel said he pounded his fist into his palm, rose quickly, knocking over his desk chair and yelled, "Damn her" several times. Then he looked right at Engel and said, "She'll pay for this! Big time! Damn her to hell!" Engel said he calmed down after pacing back and forth, mumbling something like "What am I going to do? What can I do?" The next day, when Engel returned to pick up his papers and things, he saw Truitt in the victim's office. The door was closed, but he could see her sitting behind her desk and she looked scared. And he overheard Truitt yelling and one thing he heard was "You've ruined us. How could you do this? You're going to have to pay for this." Engel said he saw that several of the staff were nearby and could overhear the same thing. Engel retrieved his things and left.

5:30 p.m: Returned to restaurant. Fingerprint reports showed those of

Truitt, several staff members on the freezer door, handle, and elsewhere in the area, but the inside of the freezer would not have produced any in any event. Made note that Ray Gotti's fingerprints were not found anywhere near the freezer or victim's office.

Friday 4/29/16

10:00 a.m: Received autopsy report. Lists hypothermia as cause of death. No time of death determinable due to body being frozen. No DNA found. It was determined that her arms had last been burned two weeks previously and the bruises on her neck and thighs a few days before she was found. Due to being frozen, it could not be determined if there were any semen in or on the body. There were no other personal items at the crime scene—no clothes, jewelry, etc. The finding that the victim's stomach was empty, meaning she hadn't eaten anything within the last two hours was not helpful because she had died some days before she was found. Nature of killing (gangland), Gotti's involvement with victim, signs on victim's arms, neck, and thighs of physical abuse, antiseptic condition of crime scene (no fingerprints, no DNA, no time of death) point to a professional job.

3:00 p.m: Went to Gotti's office. Announced he was under arrest on suspicion of murder in the death Candice Cavanaugh. Told him he had the right to remain silent and warned him that anything he said could be used against him a court of law. He immediately told his secretary to call his lawyer. Gotti taken into custody and transported to precinct headquarters.

"Yes."

"What is this document?"

It's my original investigation report that sets forth my findings and conclusions at the time."

"Thank you. We will submit for the record as Commonwealth Exhibit 8."

"You identified this as your original investigation report. Can you explain that?"

"Yes. There were two things that were later discovered. The ME's autopsy revealed that the burn marks and bruises were several weeks to a month old. Not fresh as first believed. That was a surprise. In my experience, there is usually some additional physical violence before the victim is killed or the violence would have been severe enough to cause death. A blow, or repeated blows to the head, for example. Typically, if you owe the mob and haven't paid up, you'll be roughed up; good and roughed up.

If it gets around that somebody hasn't paid or has repeatedly missed payment due dates, then it becomes necessary to send the strongest message to other deadbeats or potential deadbeats. That's when the death sentence is carried out. But the cause of death, according to the ME's autopsy, was hypothermia. She froze to death. She did not die due to recent physical violence and the burns and bruises were not life threatening."

"You said there were two things that changed your mind?"

"Yes. According to Mr. Engel's audit, Cavanaugh's last siphoning of funds was a month before her body was found. It was for $67,000. With that amount, she may have been able to pay Gotti off, or at least reduce her debt. Gotti's no fool. He wouldn't kill Cavanaugh if she could put her hands on that kind of cash."

"Did your investigation determine what happened to that $67,000?"

"We followed the trail of the funds and found she had deposited it into one of her personal bank accounts. Then she discounted that amount by writing a check for the full amount in her bank account to the Peabody Savings and Loan, taking back $62,000 and leaving Peabody with a $5,000 profit for a single transaction. We found that she had made similar transactions with the Savings and Loan on behalf of the restaurant. So, there were no questions raised."

"Were you able to determine what happened to the $62,000?"

"No. We could find no trace of it."

"Presumably it could have gone to Gotti?"

"No way to tell. When big cash comes in, the accounting system Gotti and his ilk use make Hollywood accounting seem like Bookkeeping 101."

"But if Gotti did get the cash, he would have no motive to kill Ms. Cavanaugh?"

"Objection! Calls for speculation!"

"Sustained. Move on, Ms. Payne."

"Yes, Your Honor. Detective Thornton, you were testifying about your original investigative report. Can you continue your explanation why you described that as the original report?"

"When things don't add up, I step back and review what I think I know and what I don't know. I knew Gotti was making loans to Ms. Cavanaugh. I know how those transactions can go sour to the detriment of the debtor. I would like nothing more than to have implicated him in Ms. Cavanaugh's death. But my doubts made me continue to investigate. As a result, I supplemented my original investigation report."

"I've shown you this document. Do you recognize it, Detective Thornton?"

"Yes. It's a true and accurate copy of my supplemental investigation report."

"We will mark this as Commonwealth Exhibit 9. Now, Detective, tell us what you determined as a result of your supplemental investigation."

"My further investigation focused me on the following facts. Engels had found out that Ms. Cavanaugh's embezzlements had run the partnership into the ground. Truitt became irate and threatened his partner and was overheard telling her she would get what was coming to her. For whatever reason, Gotti had staked out Buon Appetito one night. Whether that was on the night of the murder or some days before, we don't know, because we don't know when Ms. Cavanaugh died.

In any event, during his interrogation, he said he overheard the two arguing outside the kitchen's back door and saw Truitt brandishing a kitchen knife, and he appeared to be forcing Cavanaugh back up the hallway toward the kitchen.

"It wasn't until a few days later that Ms. Cavanaugh's body was found in the restaurant's freezer. Numerous impressions of the defendant's fingerprints were found on the freezer door and handles. These facts show that the defendant had the motive, the means, and the opportunity to commit the crime. His motive was anger and revenge for Cavanaugh's having ruined the business. That motive was aided by his right to receive $500,000 under the Buy-Sell agreement, which would go a long way to saving the restaurant. He had the means. Ms. Cavanaugh was found in the restaurant's freezer and died of hyperthermia, freezing to death. He had the opportunity. He had access at all times to the restaurant.

"These facts led to my conclusions to drop the charges against Gotti and charge the defendant with Cavanaugh's murder."

"Were there other things you found from your continued investigation?"

Date: Monday 05/09/16

Investigating Officer: Detective Keith Thornton

Type of Inquiry: Homicide

Address/Location: City/Town   County

14995 High Street,   Leesburg, VA 20175   Loudoun

Homicide: Nude body frozen restaurant freezer

Victim I.D.
Candice Cavanaugh, DOB 1984; Female, 5'6"; 122 lbs.; Blonde hair, blue eyes; Burn marks on left arm and hand, bruises on neck, right and left thighs.

Follow-up investigation:

05/09/16

10:00 a.m: Interrogation of Ray Gotti, suspected of mob affiliation and activities, loansharking, extortion, numbers, prostitution. Latest prior - tried for loansharking and extortion but released due to lack of evidence. Herman Michaels, Gotti's attorney, present. Gotti admits Cavanaugh owed him over $300,000 for loans made which Cavanaugh lost gambling. He explained it had gotten out of hand and no one was ever allowed to get that deep in debt. But Cavanaugh had been paying and promised to pay $100,000 within a week. Given the risk involved, Gotti admitted he tailed her to be sure she didn't suddenly get the "travel bug." He admitted he was in the alley behind the restaurant one night. Couldn't recall the exact date. But she was in the restaurant. That he knew.

He indicated that the back door is like a storm door, mostly glass. The hallway can be seen behind the door when the lights are on. This was checked and confirmed.

That night, Gotti claims he saw Truitt and Cavanaugh arguing. He moved closer so he could see if he could hear what was said. He didn't get all of what was said, but heard Truitt cursing Cavanaugh for ruining the business and that she had to pay for that. He said he couldn't be sure, but it looked like Truitt grabbed at her. In any event, she seemed to fall on him and they stood there a minute. Then they both continued up the hall toward her office. He said he knew this because he had visited Cavanaugh several times in her office.

He claims Truitt and Cavanaugh did not come out into the alley. He claims he never overheard Truitt ask Cavanaugh to go to the police to come after him to try and get some of the money back.

He decided to hang around waiting for Cavanaugh or Truitt to leave. He wanted to see Cavanaugh to see if she had the $100,000 she promised to pay him.

After about 30 minutes, Truitt left. Cavanaugh didn't leave. After Truitt left, Gotti says he went around to the front and banged on the door. No one answered. He went around to the back and tried the back door. It was locked. He thought she had to leave sometime and waited. Then he got a call and he couldn't wait any longer. He had to be someplace else. He refused to say where.

In any event, it was at least an hour and a half since Gotti saw Truitt leave and Cavanaugh had not answered the front door and was not seen in the hallway.

5/09/16

4:12 p.m: Received a call from Paul Engel, the accountant. He said he had been thinking more about the audit he had conducted and he came across something that he didn't know whether it was important or not, but decided to pass the information along. Engel said there was a Buy-Sell agreement between Truitt and Cavanaugh. He said it is a recognized practice for partnerships to have such agreements. Asked what it provided, Engel said that in case of the death of one of the partners, the surviving partner would receive insurance proceeds of $500,000.

5/10/16

10:00 a.m: After receiving a final fingerprint analysis that showed that Truitt's fingerprints were on the freezer door and handle, returned to restaurant. Truitt was in his office. Asked to see Buy-Sell agreement. Truitt produced it. As Engel said, it provided that Truitt would receive $500,000 in the event of Cavanaugh's death. Based on Gotti's statements observing Truitt and Cavanaugh in the restaurant's hallway. His interest in getting the $100,000 repayment Cavanaugh said she would make. The fingerprint analysis. Truitt's anger and threats. The Buy Sell agreement's payout of $500,000. That amount would get Truitt out of the financial hole he was in. Given these facts, Gotti was released and Truitt arrested and charged with Cavanaugh's murder.

"Well, as the County's ME explained in his testimony, there is no accurate way to establish time of death of a frozen body. So, I concentrated on looking for other things that might provide evidence that could be used to establish more clearly the circumstances of Ms. Cavanaugh's death."

"I see. Did you find anything useful?"

First, from his vantage point from behind the restaurant, Gotti says he saw Truitt with Cavanaugh on several occasions after the date Engels informed Truitt of her embezzlement and Truitt's threatening her.

On investigation of Ms. Cavanaugh's home, we found her mail box crowded. She hadn't picked up her mail for a few days. We found several voicemails recorded over a few days' time. We found her cell phone, which was odd, because people don't leave home without it, as the old credit card ad advised. But we didn't know her password, so we couldn't determine if there were voicemails or text messages on that phone."

"Were the voicemails on her home phone of any help?"

"Well, there were some odd messages. We could not identify the voices, however."

"Let me show you this document. Do you recognize it, and if so, can you tell us what it is?"

TRANSCRIPT OF VOICEMAIL MESSAGE

DECEASED'S HOME PHONE

703-333-1563 / COMMONWEALTH ATTORNEY

"Hello, Candy. You know who this is and why I'm calling. When I don't hear from you I get nervous. It's getting late. I need to hear from you. Or else."

"Hello Candy. It was nice that you dropped by in person. As you hoped, that little tumble bought you some time, but not a lot."

"Cavanaugh, where are you?"

"Ah, my sweet! Your last visit was even more stimulating and once again you have more time. But, this is the last time. Next time show up with the cash and not just yourself, or I will not be responsible for what happens. As you were told when you left, it will be far from being as pleasant as your last two visits."

"Yes. It's a transcription of the voicemails we found on Ms. Cavanaugh's phone."

"Do you also have the tape of these voicemails taken from Ms. Cavanaugh's home phone?"

"Yes, we do."

"I am handing you a brown paper bag labeled 'Evidence Bag.' Will you read what is written on it?"

"There are two bands sealing the bag and marked 'Evidence.' Then there are places to list the Attorney, the item, the case number, the date and time of collection, who created the bag, the location, suspect, victim, and then there's spaces to enter all those who handled the bag and its contents to show a proper chain of custody."

"And what is written in the spaces provided?"

"There's 'A. Payne,' for the attorney. Tape cassette, the case number of this case, the date and time this recording was made, my name as the one who created the bag, the address of the residence of the deceased, Ms. Cavanaugh. 'Unknown,' is entered into the space for the Suspect. The space for 'Victim' lists 'C. Cavanaugh.'"

"What is filled in for the chain of custody listings?"

"My name. Then officer William Brant, Property Officer. Then my name again. And finally, your name, Commonwealth's Attorney, A. Payne."

"This bag then, contains the tape of the voicemail message transcript of which you just identified?"

"Yes."

"Without objection, the Commonwealth submits the transcript identified by the witness and the voice recording tape as Exhibits 10 and 11."

"No objection."

"So ordered."

"Your Honor, the Commonwealth submits that the best evidence to show the jury would be by playing the tape. Without objection, I will do so now."

"No objection."

"Proceed counselor."

"I will place the tape in this cassette player on this table in front of the jury box and push the start button."

"Hello, Candy. You know who this is and why I'm calling. When I don't hear from you, I get nervous. It's getting late. I need to hear from you, or else."

"Hello Candy. It was nice that you dropped by in person. As you hoped, that little tumble bought you some time, but not a lot."

"Cavanaugh, where are you?"

"Ah, my sweet! Your last visit was even more stimulating and once again you have more time. But, this is the last time. Next time show up with the cash and not just yourself, or I will not be responsible for what happens. As you were told when you left, it will be far from being as pleasant as your last two visits."

"Yes, it's the diagram made around the body of the victim as she lay when we found her."

"Without objection, we will submit this as Commonwealth's Exhibit 12."

"No objection."

"So ordered."

"Does this, as you described it, show a swath from the wall where you found the letter 'a' and the two 't's?"

"Yes. The floor was dusty and we saw the arc from the wall to the victim's body."

"What, if anything, did you conclude about these markings and the swath you described?"

"Based on my experience, this is a classic example of a victim trying to identify the killer."

"Were you able to draw any conclusions as to whom she was trying to identify?"

"Not at first. But after a while it occurred to us that the defendant's surname ends in two 't's and his first name has an 'a' in it."

"We have heard that the defendant had a motive for killing Ms. Cavanaugh. What did your investigation show about means?"

"Detective Thornton, what can you tell us about the voices we just heard?"

"Even with our speech recognition technology and analytics, the fidelity of the phone tape was not good enough to identify any individual. But we did determine that the shortest message asking where Cavanaugh was, from a different speaker than the other three messages."

"What role did these tapes play, if any, in furthering your investigation?"

"At the time, our focus was on Ray Gotti. We judged that Ms. Cavanaugh was buying time by providing herself to him."

"So, even though you can't prove those three messages were left by Gotti, did they support your decision to charge him for Cavanaugh's murder?"

"Yes."

"When was the last tape recording received?"

"We can't know for sure. It's not possible to establish time of death. But given the nature of the messages, it seems clear they were recorded before Ms. Cavanaugh died. Let me correct that. They were recorded before Ms. Cavanaugh's body was found."

"What other evidence did your investigation discover?"

"It was obvious that her death was not accidentally caused. She was nude. To guard against someone accidentally locking themselves in the freezer, there is no locking mechanism on the freezer door. After someone enters, the door closes automatically to maintain the low temperature. When one wants to leave, they push down on the handle on the inside and exit. But that didn't happen here."

"Why not?"

"Truitt told us that the mechanism on the door had been malfunctioning. He showed us a trouble ticket from a firm named

'Restaurant Repair.' They had come to fix the door, but found they didn't have a part, so they had to come back to complete the repairs."

"Did they?"

"Don't know. By that I mean, they did not get back before Ms. Cavanaugh got locked into the freezer."

"When you found her body, what did you see?"

"Well, as you know, when we arrive on the scene, we assume nothing has been touched or moved. The first thing done is to photograph the scene, which was done.

When the photos of her and the floor surrounding her were taken, we looked around and saw some markings on the ice or frost coating low down on one of the walls. Some of it had melted, but there was enough to make out an 'a' and, further down, separated what looked like goal posts—that is—two lower-case 't's side by side. While she was found huddled in a fetal position, there was a swath from the point on the wall where we found the 'a' and two 't's."

"A swath, Detective Thornton?"

"Yeah, like a wiper blade removing snow. We think after she left the markings on the wall, she pulled her arm toward her body to keep warm."

"Do any of your photographs of the scene show this?"

"No. By the time we noticed this, the warmth from our presence had melted the frost containing the letters."

"Let me show you this document. Do you recognize it?"

"Well, Truitt knew that the freezer door was in need of repair. When that repair was delayed, he knew that someone could get locked in the freezer and if no one was around, would be in grave danger. Both the defendant and Cavanaugh often worked after hours when the rest of the staff had left. Truitt is a big man. Cavanaugh was average size for a woman in her early thirties. It would not be a problem for him to force her into the freezer and have her locked in due to the broken door handle."

"And opportunity?"

"Again, the murder took place in the restaurant. All the defendant had to do was wait when no one else was around and Cavanaugh was there."

"That raises another point. Once her embezzlement was discovered and she was threatened by the defendant, why wouldn't Cavanaugh just stay away from the restaurant?"

"I agree. But Cavanaugh wasn't a hardened criminal. Her crime was due to her addiction. She regretted what she had done to the business and her partner. But she was the only one that had complete knowledge of the books and records. We believe she tried to keep the financial records accurate.

"As a financial expert, she knew that those records would be needed if the partnership filed for bankruptcy. So, she came back from time to time to work on the books. She did this most of the time after hours when she thought the defendant would be gone so she did not run into him."

"This gave the defendant the opportunity he needed. We believe that it was late one evening. The restaurant would be closed and the staff gone. She went to her office, believing she was alone. Truitt confronted her. He threatened her and forced her to disrobe, or she did so to seduce him so he wouldn't harm her. When she was naked, he grabbed her and dragged her to the freezer and pushed her in, letting the door close, knowing she could not open it due to the defective safety mechanism. Knowing of her debt to Gotti, it would appear that a loan shark carried off a typical mob hit."

"But why force her to disrobe?"

"Several possibilities. Ms. Cavanaugh was an attractive woman. Truitt was divorced. He was also beside himself for what she did to the business and wanted to humiliate her in a way different from the way her bankrupting the partnership humiliated him. Besides, the staff would be returning to prepare for Saturday's service. Without clothes, she would freeze to death sooner.

"But, Truitt was careless. His fingerprints were on the outside of the freezer door. And he didn't realize there was a witness lurking in the dark shadows in the alley facing the restaurant's back door."

"Who was that?"

"Mr. Gotti."

"Why would Mr. Gotti be lurking about late at night behind the Buon Appetito?"

"He told us he did so every so often to keep an eye on her to make sure she didn't try and skip out. He watched her house at night and if she left, he'd follow her. When he did so, most of the time she went back to the restaurant.

On this particular night, he had one of his cronies keep an eye on her. Gotti's henchman followed Cavanaugh to the restaurant. When she entered, he called Gotti and waited until Gotti got there. Then he left. Gotti hung around. He thought she might be trying to get some cash or receipts out of the safe and use those to pay him off or to leave town. Since he didn't know, he staked out the restaurant."

"Did you accept Mr. Gotti's story?"

"We remained suspicious, but that disappeared when we didn't find his fingerprints anywhere in the restaurant."

"No further questions. Your witness."

"Thank you."

* * *

"Detective Thornton, you provided an impressive resume of your career. But there are other events you didn't mention, is that correct?"

"You are referring to the two times I was investigated by Internal Affairs?"

"What were those investigations about?"

"I was investigated for possible corruption and connections to the mob."

"Please tell the court and jury the specific acts that prompted those investigations?"

"They're not relevant," snapped Thornton.

"You're not the judge of that, Detective. Please tell us what those investigations were about."

"I told you. Possible corruption and connections to the mob?"

"Your Honor?"

"Detective! Answer Ms. Lyle's questions in full. Provide the details about those investigations."

"Oh, all right! I was accused of tampering with evidence to rig a case."

"What case, Detective?"

"A case involving Mr. Gotti and his brother Mario."

"What was the basis for the accusations?"

"That I intended to help them escape conviction."

"Were they convicted?"

"No."

"Why not?"

"The prosecution did not convince the jury they were guilty."

"Why was that?"

"Evidence was missing."

"What evidence?"

"Records of payoffs made to two city council members. Bribes."

"Were these records the evidence you were investigated for tampering with?"

"Yes."

"What was the basis for your being accused of having tampered with those records?"

"They went missing from the property room."

"Were you then accused of causing them to go missing?"

"That was the gist of it."

"Why were you suspected of causing then to go missing?"

"I had access to the property room where the records were kept."

"Is that all?"

"No."

"What else?"

"I was working undercover and infiltrated the mob. Doing so, I knew its members."

"And that included, Mr. Gotti and his brother?"

"Yes."

"How well did you know them?"

"I knew them."

"Did they 'know' you?"

"When you're undercover, you have to be convincing, or the infiltration won't do any good. And more importantly, you won't survive. So, they knew me."

"They trusted you, you mean?"

"Yes. That's the way it works. If you don't win their trust, you won't get the 'goods' on them."

"How much did they trust you?"

"I was pretty good at playing a local hoodlum."

"You became a member. Did you gain anything from being part of the 'family?'"

"Yeah. I got offers of women, booze, some cash."

"Did you accept these?"

"Not the women. But the booze and cash, yes."

"What happened to those things?"

"I turned them over to my superiors."

"How long were you undercover?"

"About a year and a half."

"Were you undercover when these bribes were made to the two council men?"

"Yes."

"Is that how you obtained the records of the bribes?"

"Not the actual records. I photographed them and turned those photos over."

"What happened to the originals?"

"They were destroyed."

"How?"

"Don't know. When the squad raided the mob's offices, the records weren't found."

"So, the only evidence then, were the photos of these records that you obtained when working undercover?"

"Yes. That's correct."

"Then the photos disappeared?"

"Yes."

"How?"

"I don't know. But because of my connections and access to the records, I came under suspicion."

"What were the results of the investigation?"

"Nothing. I was not indicted, not suspended. Not even

reprimanded."

"Have you maintained contacts with Mr. Gotti, his brother, or other members of his organization?"

"On and off."

"How would you describe those contacts?"

"What do you mean?"

"Were they a result of conducting other investigations of Mr. Gotti, his organization, or any of its members?"

"No, not exactly."

"Please explain."

"When Gotti and his brother were charged with bribery, it came out that I was undercover. Of course, they weren't happy about being duped. Then when the photos disappeared and the charges had to be dismissed for lack of evidence, things changed."

"How do you mean?"

"I would run into Gotti or his brother from time to time. They would say hello. Acted friendly. I didn't reciprocate, but didn't act unfriendly."

"Why?"

"I wanted to maintain contact in case something came up in the future that they may have information about. I thought it wouldn't hurt if they thought I was responsible for those photos disappearing. Most of the time, your best sources for leads to what's going on in the underworld comes from those directly involved in it."

"Is it possible, Detective, that your dropping the charges against Mr. Gotti for the murder of Ms. Cavanaugh was influenced by your previous and continuing relations with him?"

"Not at all. It's ridiculous that I would try and pin Cavanaugh's murder on the defendant to throw suspicion off of Gotti. I intend to nail Gotti for his activities. I only fingered him at first because her murder had several aspects of a mob hit. She owed

Gotti money. Despite threats and some roughing up, she hadn't been able to pay off her debt. Being iced in the freezer is typical of a mob hit."

"Do you know a Joey Lee?"

"Yeah, I know him."

"How do you know him?"

"He's a small timer. Has a long list of arrests—petty stuff. And has a few convictions. Again, small stuff. Misdemeanors."

"Have you had any contact with him recently?"

"No."

"None?"

"Not directly."

"Could you explain that?"

"I had messages left for me that he was trying to contact me."

"What about?

"Ms. Cavanaugh's murder."

"Do you know why?"

"No."

"You didn't try and find out?"

"No."

"Why not?"

"It's routine to follows all leads. But Lee's a notorious con-artist, always working on some kind of angle."

"What angle would he be looking for in this case?"

"I don't know. If I had to guess, I'd say he was trying to ingratiate himself by attempting to look helpful so he could use that the next time he was busted."

"What if he had information that implicated Mr. Gotti in Ms. Cavanaugh's murder?"

"If I thought he did, I would have talked to him of course. But, my experience, and what I had already decided about what the facts showed, I knew talking to Lee was a waste of time. And I had this and other open cases on my agenda. I didn't want to waste time on Lee."

"But if he did have relevant information, and it concerned Mr. Gotti, yet you ignored him, then given your history with Gotti, isn't that suspicious?"

"Suspicious of what?"

"Come on, Detective! Gotti got off on a case you worked because evidence went missing. You were investigated by Internal Affairs for tampering with that evidence on the theory that you wanted to help Gotti beat the rap. And Gotti did beat the rap. Now, you first charged Gotti as the murderer in this case, only to drop those charges in favor of accusing my client, Mr. Truitt. And Gotti provided information that is incriminating to my client. You don't think these circumstances suggest your protecting Mr. Gotti again?"

"I stand by the evidence. We did not find Mr. Gotti's fingerprints anywhere at the site of the murder. Cavanaugh may have been late on her payments, but she still had the means to make further pay backs. If Gotti did threaten her, that's standard. But we have no evidence he intended to kill her. The fact that she had been roughed up was enough to scare her. She knew she had to repay Gotti, and Gotti knew this too."

"Okay. Let's sum up here. You have had a relationship with Gotti. You admit that in that relationship you played your undercover part so well that Gotti trusted you. That you at times had difficulty remembering you were just acting the part. Then Gotti's tried for bribery and the evidence against him goes missing. Consequently, Gotti gets off. You're investigated for being responsible for losing the evidence, but that can't be proved. Gotti goes back to his racketeering, you maintain some relationship with him.

Then Cavanaugh is murdered gangland-style and you conclude Gotti's responsible. But then, you change your mind and drop the case against Gotti and charge my client. Once again, Gotti gets off the hook and you're mainly responsible for that. Doesn't all this seem a little too coincidental? Even to you?"

"No. You're just trying to discredit me, which is no surprise to me."

"Really, Detective? No further questions."

CHAPTER 5

Witness For The Prosecution

Ray Gotti

"The prosecution calls Raymond Gotti to the stand."

"Please raise your right hand. Do you swear to tell the truth, the whole truth, and nothing but the truth?"

"I do."

"Please state your name for the record."

"My name is Raymond Gotti."

"And what do you do for a living, Mr. Gotti?"

"Mostly, I loan money to people and those loans are interest bearing—just like a bank."

"To whom do you loan money?"

"People that are not able to get a conventional loan from a bank or other mainstream financial institution."

"You mean like those companies that offer loans based on car titles?"

"Yeah, like dat. But different."

"How so?"

"Those car title people are small-change operations."

"What do you mean?"

"Their loans are for chump change amounts. We've all seen the ads—$1,000, $2,500, $10,000. The last amount is the highest I've seen offered."

"You offer larger loans?"

"Oh yes! Much larger."

"How much larger, for example?"

"It depends on the circumstances, but in general they range from five to six figures."

"Can you tell us what would be some of the circumstances?"

"First, it depends on who needs the loan. The person. Then, what amount is needed. After that, what's the loan for. Why is it needed? Then, the biggest factor is whether the person is good for it. You know! Has access to resources to pay back the loan, plus the interest."

"Are your lending activities regulated like banks and other institutions?"

"No. We don't hold ourselves out to make loans. It's all done privately. People come to us. We don't solicit. It's like asking a family member or a friend for a loan. Those types of loans aren't regulated either."

"You mentioned you check to see if the person can pay back the loan and interest. What interest rates do you charge?"

"Whatever we think the traffic will bear. Usually, it's higher than what your major credit cards charge."

"Well, those run as high as 20–25%. Are yours higher?"

"Generally, yes."

"Why is that?"

"Like I said. We don't seek out customers. They come to us. They can't get a conventional loan in the amount they need at any interest rate."

"How much higher?"

"Now that's a trade secret! I won't answer that."

"How did you get into the lending business?"

"It's a family business. I've been in it since high school. Didn't need college."

"Lending money? Especially in large sums is risky and complicated, isn't it?"

"For some, I guess. But the way we run the family business, we keep it simple. We offer services and get paid for those services."

"But what about all the documentation that is part of the lending business? Liens, promissory notes, UCC Forms?"

"We don't use any of those. Those that borrow from us know they owe us. When we lend them money they know we expect to be paid. In full! Plus interest! If a client doesn't pay, he or she gets a firm reminder. And like that [snaps fingers] they pay up. We are very persuasive."

"What was it about Ms. Cavanaugh that qualified her for loans from you?"

"She had a solid job, was a partner in a restaurant I knew was doing pretty well. Didn't hurt she was a 'looker,' if you know what I mean. Anyway, we started out slow with her and she repaid on time with interest. When one does that, we're ready to make additional loans."

"In larger amounts?"

"Yeah. It increases the profits we make on the interest."

"Did you ask why she needed the loans?"

"Not at first."

"But later?"

"Yeah."

"Why?"

"Payments were late and did not include the interest at times. Those are bad signs. So, we asked her what she needed the money for and why she needed larger loans."

"What did she tell you?"

"We finally got it out of her. She liked to gamble. A lot!"

"You knew she was borrowing the funds to gamble?"

"Yeah."

"Didn't you consider that high risk?"

"We checked her out. We have connections in that area. Like most gamblers, she would have a winning streak, then a slump. But she was ahead of the game most of the time."

"But her luck ran out?"

"Yeah, about six months ago."

"She was losing over that period of time?"

"Not always. But her wins were not big enough to cover her losses."

"She fell behind?" "Yeah! Big time!"

"You started putting pressure on her. Like you said, when you let people know they owe you, they pay up."

"Most of the time. Yeah!"

"What do you know about the burn marks found on her body?"

"Nothin."

"What about the bruises found on her body?"

"Same answer. Nothin."

"In what way do you let your 'clients' know they owe you so they pay up?"

"The usual ways."

"What are those?"

"You know. You hassle them. Call 'em on the phone. Send demand letters. Visit with them to emphasize the point."

"When you 'visit' them, what do you do exactly?"

"Hey! Just showing up. Being face to face. Making the demand in person."

"That's all? No 'rough play'?"

"Hey! I ain't no loan shark. They're with da mob. I'm not."

"You know the mob?

"Look, attorney! All I know about the mob I learned from

watching movies."

"Were you aware the police at first thought Cavanaugh was murdered by the mob? That being 'iced' as she was, was typical of a mob hit?"

"I know nothin' about how the mob operates. Of course, I heard they thought the mob was involved, but since I'm not a mobster, I don't know why they charged me."

"You were at the Buon Appetito the same night before Ms. Cavanaugh's body was found, is that correct?"

"Yeah, I was there."

"Why?"

"I'd been following Cavanaugh for a few weeks. One night, I decided to check up on her and went to the restaurant and went around to the alley behind the restaurant and waited."

"Why go back there?"

"I didn't know if she knew I was tailing her. But you have to play hunches in this game. I assumed she may have spotted me. If she had, then it was likely she might try and evade me by sneaking out the back way. I staked the joint out from across the back door to the kitchen that opens onto the alley. I almost blew it. Because when I came around the corner to enter the alley, Cavanaugh was outside smoking a cigarette. After she went back in, I set up across from the back door behind the dumpsters."

"Go on, please."

"I was getting nervous. I'd been there a while and it was after hours. I thought everyone had left and she left with them so I couldn't confront her. But to my surprise, she and Truitt came storming out of the back door of the kitchen. They were arguing. Truitt grabbed her arm and twirled her around. She tried to break free, but Truitt's a big guy and held on. She said, 'you're hurting me, let go.' He yanked her arm and she yelled, 'Ow! You bastard.'"

"Then what happened?"

"Truitt yelled back. 'Me? Me? I'm the bastard? You bitch! You stole from your own partner. You bankrupted the business. The restaurant will close and the employees will lose their jobs.'"

"At that, she started crying. I think I heard her say she was sorry. She said it in a low voice, but I'm pretty sure that was what she said."

"Go on."

"When I heard what Truitt said, I realized she was getting the money from the restaurant to pay me.

"Yes?"

"He let go of her arm and I saw a gleam from something in his right hand. Whatever it was, he pointed it at Cavanaugh and shoved her toward the back door. They both went inside."

"Did you witness anything after they went back in?"

"Yeah."

"Isn't the back door itself is solid wood or metal."

"I don't know. But there's a storm door that has a full-length glass pane. The lights were still on in the hallway and I could see Truitt pushing her along up the hall. The kitchen was on their right and the seating area on their left, so I think he must have been forcing her toward the offices."

"Did Cavanaugh or Truitt see you at any time?"

"No. Not to my knowledge."

"How did you know the man was Truitt? Had you seen him before?"

"Yeah. At the beginning, I would occasionally pick up Cavanaugh's payments at the restaurant. I saw this big guy sitting in the office next to Cavanaugh's. It was the same big guy I saw arguing with Cavanaugh in the alley that night."

"After they went back into the restaurant, what did you do?"

"I waited. But it occurred to me that this was not a good time to confront Cavanaugh about being late on her payments. Still, I decided to wait a bit. I saw Truitt come out the back door, walk down the alley and get into a car parked in the street and drive off. I thought I might have a chance to confront Cavanaugh after all, with Truitt gone. But, the back door was locked. I banged on it. No answer. I went around front. Everything was dark inside. Front door was locked. I banged on it. No answer. I gave up and left. When I was picked up on suspicion I had something to do with Cavanaugh's murder, I told the cops what I just told you all."

"Your witness, counsel."

* * *

"Mr. Gotti, Detective Thornton was responsible for dropping the charges against you. You and he have a history. Isn't that right?"

"History? Don't know what that means. But yeah, I know Thornton."

"Are you testifying because you know Detective Thornton?"

"No!"

"Why are you testifying?"

"I'm testifying. Telling what I know."

"That the only reason?"

"Yeah!"

"Come now, Mr. Gotti! Don't play dumb. You're testifying because you made a deal with the prosecution. What was it?"

"Oh, all right! There was an investigation into my dealings with Cavanaugh."

"You mean your loans to her?"

"Yeah!

"What was the basis for the investigation?"

"Loan sharking."

"When did you learn you were being investigated for loan

sharking?"

"I don't recall."

"It was after Detective Thornton dropped his charges against you and charged Mr. Truitt, wasn't it?"

"If you say so."

"Your Honor?"

"Answer the question, Mr. Gotti."

"Yes."

"Why should the jury believe you, Mr. Gotti?"

"I got no reason to lie. I won't commit perjury!"

"Very wise, Mr. Gotti. But lying is not really the issue. What is at issue is your credibility. What you saw, what you did, and the motivations for your testimony."

"I'm helping out here!"

"Is it true you've had a rap sheet starting when you were a juvenile?"

"Yeah."

"Were you convicted of theft?

"Yeah. It was for less than $1,500 and all I had to do was work with a road crew."

"You had a second conviction not too much later?"

"I forget."

"I have the record here. Do I need to show you to refresh your memory?"

[After a pause.] "Nah."

"It's for an assault in the second degree."

"No big deal. I got a suspended sentence and was on probation for a year."

"After that?"

"It was a lot of years later. Six or seven."

"What were you convicted of?"

"It was for extortion."

"What was your sentence?"

"I did over a year in the slammer."

"Were there other charges brought against you?"

"I was charged with bribery."

"That's the case that involved Detective Thornton. The one that led to Thornton's being accused of tampering with evidence. Is that correct?"

"Yes. But he wasn't…"

"That's enough, Mr. Gotti. We have to move on. You testified you don't use physical force to collect from those who owe you money. Do you recall that?"

"Yeah."

"Were you ever charged with threatening a man by the name of Art Perkins? Remember, you're under oath."

"Yeah."

"What do you remember?"

"I was charged with threatening the guy because he owed me money."

"What was the nature of the threat you made?

"I don't follow."

"Well, did you threaten to sue to recover what you were owed?"

"No."

"Foreclose on some collateral you had to secure the loan?"

"No."

"Isn't it true you threatened to 'whack his knees with a baseball bat?'"

"Yeah."

"Were you tried?"

"Yeah."

"What happened?"

"The case got thrown out."

"Why?"

"The prosecution's key witness didn't show up and couldn't be found."

"Was the witness ever found?"

"Oh yes."

"Where?"

"He was somewhere in Europe."

"On another occasion, you were charged with assault. Is that correct?"

"Yeah."

"The charge is still pending?"

"Yeah."

"What was the nature of the assault?"

"I was accused of trying to strangle some guy."

"Mr. Gotti. You claim to be a business man providing services. More specifically, loans. You claim those loans are repaid with interest. You claim you don't need to resort to violence to get those loans repaid. But your record suggests otherwise. Isn't it true, Mr. Gotti, that Ms. Cavanaugh became seriously delinquent in her payments? That word had got around that you were taking it easy on her because you demanded sexual favors?"

"No."

"Isn't it true that you became worried about allowing Ms. Cavanaugh to delay repayment. That you decided you had to do something to send a message that you weren't getting soft?"

"No."

"Isn't it true that the night you followed Ms. Cavanaugh to Buon Appetito and waited outside in the alley until Mr. Truitt left, that you then went into the restaurant and found her in her office?"

"No."

"Then you demanded she pay up, or else?"

"No."

"She offered herself to you once again to calm you down. You played along. You had plenty of time. You got her drinking."

"No."

"When she was intoxicated, you made her disrobe. You raped her. When you finished, you forced her, naked, into the freezer. Shoved her in and slammed the door. When word got out on the street what happened to her, those in debt to you would learn about it. Your reputation would be restored, right?"

"No! You can't pin Cavanaugh's murder on me. No way. I have a record. I may have used some strong-arm tactics now and then. But I never murdered nobody. Why would I kill her? She had a track record of paying what she owed. Sure, I was keepin' tabs on her. I was worried she might try and skip out on me. With a gambler like her, she could leave at any time to look for a big score. She was addicted. Couldn't stay away from the action. When she had a run of good luck, she got cocky. The curse of gamblers like her. I knew at times she would gamble six days a week, eight hours a day for several weeks and lose big money. Perhaps her biggest problem was she was good at gambling. But no matter how good, the more you play the more often the 'house' wins."

"When she died, how much did Ms. Cavanaugh owe you?"

"She owed me over $200,000. But she made good on nearly $300,000 before that."

"Did you think she repaid you with her winnings?"

"I never thought about it. I never concerned myself with where Cavanaugh got her money."

"That's surprising, Mr. Gotti."

"Why?"

"Let me ask you this. If you knew she was embezzling to cover her bets and losses, would that be a concern to you?"

"No! Why should it?"

"You don't see any irony in her paying back gambling debts by stealing the money?"

"Irony? What's that mean?"

"Mr. Gotti, when you found out she had been embezzling from the partnership to gamble and pay your loans, you panicked. You knew that she would never get the money to pay what she owed because she had tapped out her source of funds by bankrupting the restaurant.

Moreover, once she was found out, she would be arrested, tried, and convicted, leaving you holding the bag. But even worse, you would look stupid. You'd lose street cred. Big time. And you couldn't allow that without risking defaults on other delinquent loans. And that's why you followed her to the restaurant that night. Waited until Mr. Truitt left. Then took care of your problem. Sending a message that you are not to be messed with. And if you are, the price tag is death."

"No! No! I didn't even know she was bilking the restaurant until that night! Like I said, when I overheard she and Truitt arguing in the alley."

"You really expect us to believe that? You had to know where she was getting the money because you don't let late payments go without finding out what's going on. She could be winning and keeping her winnings. She could be losing big and never be able to pay you back. With a six-figure debt you would not just sit there and do nothing. And indeed, if that were true, your street cred still takes a big hit."

"I... I just figured she had an ace in the hole."

"Really? Where would she get that? Did you investigate? Just assumed she did? You want us to believe that one can be cavalier in the loan sharking business?"

"I'm not a loan shark!"

"So you have said."

"Do you know Joey Lee?"

"Yeah! I know him."

"He'll be testifying for the defense. Do you want to tell us anything before he does? You might make it easier on yourself."

"Lee's a liar. If he told you anything about me and Cavanaugh, it's a lie. Lee's way of getting some deal on whatever it is he's up for. Or he thought I'd be willing to pay some hush money. If he did, he got fooled when the charges against me on Cavanaugh's murder were dropped."

"Interesting, Mr. Gotti. Why would Mr. Lee think you would pay him hush money?"

"He's always looking for an easy buck. Besides, my arrest for Cavanaugh's murder was all over the news. He's a liar, but no dummy. He thought he had me in a tight spot."

"Okay, Mr. Gotti, we'll leave it there for now. No further questions."

"Redirect, Ms. Payne?"

"No, your Honor, but we reserve the right to recall Mr. Gotti."

"Duly noted."

"The prosecution rests."

"Very well. Ms. Lyle, call your first witness."

CHAPTER 6

Witness For The Defense
Carl Truitt

"The defense calls Carl Truitt."

"Mr. Truitt, please raise your right hand. Do you swear to tell the truth, the whole truth, and nothing but the truth?"

"Yes."

"Please be seated."

"You may proceed, Ms. Lyle."

"Thank you, Your Honor."

"Please state your name and occupation for the record."

"My name is Carl Truitt. I am—was—a partner in the Buon Appetito restaurant."

"Ms. Candice Cavanaugh was your former partner?"

"Yes."

"Did you kill Ms. Cavanaugh?"

"No."

"Can you briefly summarize your background before you formed your partnership with Ms. Cavanaugh?"

"Yes. The reason I got into the restaurant business was because I grew up on a farm. We grew a lot of different crops and raised pigs and chickens. What we didn't sell, or decided not to sell, we kept for ourselves. Anyway, my life on the farm sparked my interest in cooking and thinking about becoming a chef. I took jobs in restaurants and worked my way up until I was preparing the dishes on the menus. I got some formal training that allowed me to go to a bigger city and work in more upscale restaurants. Long story short, I had enough experience and saved enough money to qualify for a Small Business Administration loan to open my own restaurant.

"But the one thing missing was my lack of a business background. Most importantly in the areas of finance and accounting. But the SBA has a program that puts people like me in contact with people who have the expertise in the areas I was not good at. The flip side of that is the challenge of finding a person with the expertise I needed who was looking for the type of role I had. That's how I met Ms. Cavanaugh. She was a CPA and was looking for an opportunity to partner in a business where she could handle the books and finances.

"We met, and she had some background in the management and finances of a restaurant business. She had her CPA license. Had practiced with some accounting firms and wanted to lend her skills to a business in which she had an ownership interest. Because we had complimentary talents and would be investing the same amount of funds, we agreed we would each own half of the partnership. That's how we got started.

"With Ms. Cavanagh handling all the financial aspects of the business, I was free to create the cuisine we would serve, envision the décor of the restaurant, and hire the right wait staff, sous chef, and other kitchen staff.

The first year was tough. But we managed to get through it in no small part because of her management of the finances. The second year, we made real progress but were not yet out of the woods. Nevertheless, it pointed to the third year as the one that would establish the restaurant on a firm footing. I thought we had a promising future."

"You never had any indication about Ms. Cavanaugh's gambling?"

"No. We didn't socialize. We only saw each other at work. She would come in for normal work hours. Not restaurant hours."

"What does that mean?"

"Her work dovetailed regular business hours, even banking hours. She would come in the morning and leave at a regular closing hours; five or six o'clock unless there was some reason to work late."

"What kind of reasons might those be?"

"Year-end accounting. Taxes. Auditing large orders of supplies. Comparing prices on wines. That sort of thing."

"You never asked about the accounting or finances?"

"Well, in hindsight, I should have paid attention to the finances. But, that was why she was my partner. I just didn't want to be bothered with books and records. I wanted to prepare the cuisine and make sure we offered our guests the best cuisine in the area. To me, that spelled ultimate success and she and I would make money. Me doing what I loved. She doing what she was expert at. It seemed like a perfect partnership."

"How did the Buy-Sell agreement come about?"

"It was her suggestion. She explained it could be funded by insurance. She explained that it was a necessary precaution. She said not planning for the unthinkable that one believes will never happen has ruined many a good business. Having it in place, and never having to use it doesn't cost anything. Not having it in place when something tragic happens can be financially disastrous, she said. Made sense to me. So, we made the agreement. She took care of all the details. She told me that cash flow would easily cover the premiums."

"Did you read any of the terms of the policy?"

"I did. There's nothing more boring than reading an insurance policy. But I forced myself to do so."

"When you did, what did you find out?"

"Well, what I remember is, number one, the payout was $500,000. The premium was reasonable. And one last thing. There's no payout if one of us is involved in the death of the other."

"You mean causing the death?"

"Yes."

"If you murdered Ms. Cavanaugh, you don't get the pay out?"

"That's right."

"But you were angry when you found she had bankrupted the company. You threatened her."

"Yes, I did. But that came from the shock. After everything we had built together, she betrayed me. The business. Destroyed a bright future. I was beside myself. I don't think anyone would have reacted differently. But it was an idle threat. I've never even hit anyone in anger. There's no way I could have forced her into that freezer with no clothes on and left her to die. Heck, when I calmed down, I remember we had the buy-sell in place because of her that could save the business. Now, I think of her insistence on having the buy-sell as making up for ruining the business."

"Do you think she insisted because she was aware of her gambling addiction and that she could use the partnership funds to feed it?"

"I don't know. But my understanding is that people with the addiction are confident they will win more than they lose."

"What difference to you does that make?"

"Well, given that she convinced herself she would win enough to replenish what she stole, she would not see her using partnership funds as a betrayal. Other than this addiction, she was dedicated to making the restaurant a success."

"It sounds, Mr. Truitt, that you have forgiven Ms. Cavanaugh."

"I don't know about that. This never should have happened. Even with the buy-sell, it's not certain the restaurant will recover.

It will be closed for a long time. It will lose the reputation it had built. I will need to start over. Rename the restaurant. Try and overcome the bad vibes created by a murder having taken place on the premises. I'm far from being out of the woods. Not to mention the loss of all the hard work and good will over the last three years."

"You had no idea of the financial condition of the partnership until just before Ms. Cavanaugh was killed?"

"Yes, that's correct. I was stunned when she told me we were in trouble. We were booked solid most nights and even the luncheon traffic was steady.

"My first thought was that I needed to understand why. When I asked her, she gave me generalized answers that didn't make sense. That made me suspicious, but not understanding accounting, I couldn't call her on it. I called the local SBA office. They told me I should hire an independent accountant, preferably a forensic accountant. They had to explain what that meant. When I did understand, I asked if they could recommend one. They gave me three names and contact information. The first one I called was not taking on new clients right then. The second said they would get back to me. The third one I called was the one who had the time, the credentials, and was ready to start working immediately."

"That would be Mr. Paul Engel?"

"Yes. When I explained why I was seeking outside review of the company accounts and that it was for a restaurant, he mentioned he had experience in the area. He said some common areas that could be problems were with our suppliers, our 'per-plate costs' versus our 'per-plate pricing,' and other things that told me this was the expert I needed. The last thing he told me shocked me."

"What was that?"

"He said that in the restaurant business, in particular, there was a lot of opportunity for employee theft. At the time, I took this to mean that some employees were taking some of our food stuffs, wines, beers, glasses, silverware, and such."

"You didn't suspect Ms. Cavanaugh was at fault?"

"No. Never even occurred to me."

"What then?"

"The next day, after I hired Mr. Engel, I purchased a key and padlock to secure our supplies in the freezer, the pantry, and storage room where we kept the table setting items. Ms. Cavanaugh asked me about the locks and when I told her why, she said it was a good idea."

"When did Mr. Engel begin his audit?"

"He came two days after our initial conversation."

"What did he do?"

"He did a quick overview of the premises and the books. He said he could take on the task, but that it would take a few weeks to complete both because of the amount of work needed and the need for him to work on other matters for other clients."

"I asked about the cost and he quoted me a rate of $15,000 that had to be paid upfront."

"Did you?"

"At first, I was taken aback, but he explained that if the restaurant was in serious financial trouble, he risked not being paid after he had done the work. I saw his point and paid him out of my own pocket."

"You didn't consult Ms. Cavanaugh?"

"No. That wasn't intentional. I was so upset and relieved to have found someone who could help, I hired him on the spot."

"When did she know Mr. Engel would be auditing the books?"

"The day he showed up to start the audit. When I explained, she didn't seem nervous, concerned, or suspicious. Then I realized, she never shows any emotion or concern when there's something unexpected or a surprise."

"What happened next?"

"Business went on as usual those next two weeks during the audit. Ms. Cavanaugh worked her regular hours, as did I. On the last day of the two-week period, Engel came into my office and shut the door. He looked grim. He told me I better sit down."

"What did he tell you?"

"He said he discovered why we were in the red. But then he floored me by telling me it was due to Ms. Cavanaugh's control of the money. I asked him to spell it out. He was curiously reluctant and sat there a minute, which seemed like an hour. I said, 'What do you mean?' And he told me the unthinkable. She had embezzled partnership funds. I jumped up and said, 'What? How much?' And he told me the amount was over $300,000! I was stunned! I fell back into my chair and just sat there for a minute or two. I didn't understand. This was her business too. Stealing from it was stealing from herself, as well as me, and the employees!"

"What happened next?"

"Engel asked me what I was going to do. I said I didn't know and asked him what I could do. He asked if the firm had insurance covering theft. I said I didn't know. If we did, Ms. Cavanaugh would have arranged it. But since she never mentioned it, I doubted it."

"Please continue."

"Engel rose, offered his hand. I shook it and he said he was sorry and left. I sat down again. I started to think. The more I did, the madder I got. Then I tried to get control, talked to myself. I recalled her family had money. And since I didn't know at the time what she had done with the money, I thought when confronted she might still have some of the money and having been caught, could give some back.

"I picked up my phone and called her office and forced myself to keep in control. When she answered, I struggled to keep my voice under control. I asked if she could come to my office. She said she was in the middle of something and asked if it was important. I kept control and told her it was more important than anything she was working on at that moment. She said okay. We hung up and a few minutes later she entered my office. I looked at her, and then, I'm afraid I lost control. I didn't ask her to shut the door, sit down, or anything. I just blurted out, 'What have you done? Why have you done this?'

"She's a cool one. She just asked what I was talking about. I looked at her and shouted, 'You stole from this company! You've bankrupted it. I'll see that you pay for this! How could you? How could you?' Once I started, I couldn't control it. I just yelled and shouted at her. I was beside myself with anger. She just stood there and looked at me. Didn't say anything. Didn't apologize, didn't say I was mistaken; that I didn't know what I was talking about. She just stood there looking at me. That made me even angrier. So, I said things I regret."

"Did you threaten to kill her?"

"Probably. I was certainly angry enough to do so. I felt so betrayed."

"I've asked before, but I'll ask again. Did you kill her?"

"No!"

"Did she ever explain to you what she did with the money?"

"No. After I finished ranting and raving, she apologized, then she turned and left my office. I was in disbelief. She not only didn't deny she stole, she offered no excuses; didn't offer to make it up to me. I noticed that the staff was outside my office and looked stunned. She walked past them to her office and shut the door.

The staff stood there for a moment and was about to break up. I hurried out from behind my desk and told them to wait. They stopped and turned toward me. I told them I was sorry they had to hear all that. I told them we would be re-opening for the supper crowd in a couple of hours and we needed to be ready to serve our customers. They looked at me like I was demented. But after a few minutes, they nodded and returned to their duties. I went back into my office, got that night's menu, and went to the kitchen to help prepare the dishes we would be offering. I don't know when Ms. Cavanaugh left the restaurant. One of the staff said she had seen her leave about a half-hour after I confronted her."

"Let's be clear. After your confrontation with Ms. Cavanaugh, your thinking was that she had or might have the resources to restore some of the money she embezzled?"

"Yes. I was desperate. I had to cling to any hope that something could still be done. Something at least to reduce the damage."

"In that mindset, it would be counterproductive to murder Ms. Cavanaugh, no?"

"Objection, Your Honor! Leading the witness."

"Sustained."

"Did you eventually learn that she used the money she embezzled to fund her gambling addiction?"

"Yes."

"When was that, or how did you find out?"

"It was some days later. I questioned my staff about anything they might have seen or heard that might have a connection with what had happened. Several of them remembered seeing a man that came to her office. When he did, the door was shut. When he left, it was noticed that she seemed tense. After a few visits like that, one of the staff came to me and said he thought the man looked familiar.

"He decided to check his suspicion and looked up the name of the man he thought was the one who had come to see Ms. Cavanaugh those times. He looked up Ray Gotti and got a positive identification. My employee told me that Mr. Gotti was thought to be connected to organized crime—loan sharking in particular. He also said the 'loans' Mr. Gotti arranged were often to cover gambling losses. When I learned this, my heart sank. I knew if that were true, the possibility of any recovery would be out the window."

"What did you do?"

"I had my employee visit some of the local casinos with a picture of Ms. Cavanaugh. She was identified at several. There was no other conclusion then that she had used the firm's money to gamble."

"What, if any, conclusions did you draw from this information?"

"The money—all the money—was gone."

"Then what did you do?"

"She was in her office. The staff was cleaning up after the last serving. Everyone else was gone. I asked her to come to my office. When she got there, I told her what I knew. She broke down and admitted she gambled. When I pressed her, she admitted she was addicted. Couldn't stop.

"Over the last several months she had sustained heavy losses and needed money to keep gambling and win back what had been lost. The only place she could get money was Ray Gotti, a known loan shark. She referred to him as 'Mr. Gotti' and told me she owed him over $250,000. She said she had already paid him over $300,000, all of which came from the restaurant. She tried to borrow from her family, but they refused. Then she told me that Gotti threatened to kill her if she didn't come up with the money. She claimed Gotti got rough with her—choked her, burned her arms with cigarettes. She even admitted she had sex with him to buy time."

"Do you recall your reaction when she told you these things for the first time?"

"Yes. At first, I couldn't help feeling sorry for her. But then I thought about what she had done. To satisfy her compulsion to gamble, she stole from the business. She did it repeatedly and used the firm's money to pay off Gotti so she could gamble some more. All that money she used was gone forever. We could never get a penny back. She bankrupted us—ruined what we had worked so hard and long for.

"Not once did she ask for help. Never did she reveal her addiction. When these thoughts hit me, I didn't feel sorry anymore. I was stunned. Then I got angry. Angier than I have ever been before in my life. I started to yell at her. I couldn't stop. The frustration and disappointment welled up. I threatened her. Yes, if I had had a gun or a knife then, I might have killed her right then and there. But I didn't."

"What did you do then?"

"I stood there a few minutes and said nothing. She said nothing. Then I asked if she had any records of what she paid Gotti. She asked me why I was asking. I said we could go to the police and charge him with loan sharking. If he was arrested and charged, we might have a claim to get the money back; at least the excessive interest he charged.

"She looked at me with a hint of a smile. It was a sad smile. Then she said if she ratted out Gotti, she'd be the only witness of their dealings. The only witness of what she had to pay him. The only witness who knew the exorbitant interest he charged. She said he'd deny everything. She said that when they began, Gotti made a point of telling her that he keeps no records of his loans. She'd have nothing to support her accusations. But once having accused him, he would have to react. And his reaction would be violent and likely deadly. I said something like, 'Well, you got yourself into this, why should I care how you get out of it?'"

"How did she react? Did she say anything?"

"She ran out of the office. The staff was outside my office, cleaning up and organizing for the next day. It was obvious they overheard us. To get away from their stares, she turned and went down the hallway leading to the back door and the alley. I followed her out into the alley. I yelled, 'Where do you think you're going?' I said, 'You have to go to the police. You must tell them about Gotti. It's our only chance to get some money back.' She turned around and I saw she was crying. I grabbed her arm when she tried to pass me. I spun her around and demanded that we go to the police. She pulled free and said Gotti would kill her. Then she turned and went back into the restaurant."

"Did you see anyone or anything else at the time?"

"Yes. I noticed someone standing beside the dumpster that's in the alley. I think he knew I spotted him because he moved back into the shadows."

"It was a man?"

"Yes. A man."

"What did you do after Ms. Cavanaugh went back into the restaurant?"

"I followed her. Caught up to her in the hallway. Grabbed her arm and spun her around and she fell against me. I had to put my arms around her to prevent both of us from falling. When I did, I felt her trembling. I don't know why, but I continued to hold her for a few minutes. Then I released her and she went back to her office. I followed. She sat down behind her desk and stared straight ahead, not looking at me. She said not a word."

"Did you take her unresponsiveness as defiance?"

"No. She seemed defeated."

"What did you do next?"

"I gave up. I mean, I saw no point in carrying on the conversation. I went back to my office and got my keys, intending to leave the restaurant and drive home."

"Did you?"

"Yes."

"You stayed there? At home, I mean."

"Yes. All night."

"Anyone with you?"

"No. I live alone."

"Let's go back a minute to the alley. You're saying that someone was in the alley when you and Ms. Cavanaugh were arguing. Mr. Gotti's testimony confirms he was the man you saw."

"That's right."

"It also means he overheard you telling Ms. Cavanaugh to turn him in. He saw you and her when you went back into the hallway. From his vantage point, when you caught Ms. Cavanaugh, would it have looked like you were embracing her?"

"Because she was trembling, my action was non-thinking—spontaneous. But to anyone observing us, it would look like an embrace. It did to some of the staff that were still standing around."

"How do you know that?"

"When I was leaving, the employee who told me about Gotti stopped me and asked if I was still angry with Ms. Cavanaugh. I said, 'If you mean that incident just now in the hallway, it was an accident. Nothing else.'"

"Mr. Gotti testified that when you and Ms. Cavanaugh went back into the hallway, you were brandishing a knife, threatening Ms. Cavanaugh."

"That's a lie."

"But your fingerprints were found on a kitchen knife."

"Of course! They're all over the knives and spoons and other cookware because I use them all when preparing what we serve."

"Ms. Cavanaugh died from hyperthermia."

"Yes, that's my understanding."

"Then, what about Mr. Gotti's assertion you had a kitchen knife when he saw you in the hallway with Ms. Cavanaugh and you used it to force her into the freezer?"

"I don't know. It makes no sense. Unless he made the statement to throw suspicion on to me."

"When did you last see Ms. Cavanaugh that evening? The evening you argued over going to the police?"

"The last time I saw her was about 11:30 p.m. She was still in her office. I don't know why or what she was doing."

"What else do you recall about that evening?"

"When I got home, I remembered I had forgotten to lock up."

"Lock up?"

"Yes. I lock up the freezer and the back door to the alley. The doors at the main entrance self-lock. And I left by that exit. Anyway, I was about to go back and do so. Then I thought, why bother? The losses weren't due to employee theft. And I just couldn't at that moment face going back to the restaurant. Especially since I knew she might still be there."

"Would anyone else have been able to lock up the freezer or back door?"

"No. I have the only keys in order to avoid employees stealing from the restaurant."

"So, both the freezer and back door were left open?"

"Yes."

"And when you left, Ms. Cavanaugh was still in her office?"

"Yes."

"You were at home and didn't leave?"

"Yes."

"When did you leave your house after this night?"

"The next morning. Late morning. I had trouble falling asleep because of what had happened. When I finally fell asleep, I overslept and didn't wake until about 9:30 a.m. I'm usually up by six. I jumped out of bed and hurried to get ready. I must be at the restaurant at least two hours before we open for lunch at 11:30 a.m. I had already missed that deadline. Then I remembered I had hung the 'Closed' sign when I left, as I usually do."

"You hang that sign on the front entrance?"

"Yes. That's why I leave by the front entrance. Anyway, I didn't have to worry about getting ready to serve luncheon that day. But the staff would still arrive and would have to remain outside until I got there. Since I was going to be late, I called my head waiter. Told him I was running late, but I had accidentally left the back-door unlocked. I told him that he and the rest of the staff could get in that way or come back later, as we would remain closed until I got there."

"So you did go to the restaurant that day?"

"Yes, but I was in no hurry at that point, since we don't begin prepping for the dinner crowd until around 3:30."

"What time did you arrive that day?"

"A little before three. I had decided to give myself some more time before I went back. I suppose I was afraid of running into Candy… Ms. Cavanaugh. Just thinking about her at the time got me mad again and I didn't want any more scenes. I knew it wouldn't change anything."

"What happened after you did return?"

"I saw that most of the staff was already there. They were beginning the preparation for dinner service. When I saw them, my heart sank. I knew we could continue to operate for a few more days, but then we would have to order fresh provisions and we didn't have the money to pay for them. I also didn't have the money to pay the staff. I called the staff together and told them that we wouldn't be opening this evening or anytime soon, if ever. Then I told them that they were free to look elsewhere, as I had no money to pay them beyond the last few days. And I would have to use my own funds to do so."

"Was Ms. Cavanaugh there?"

"No."

"What happened next? After you told the staff?"

"They came up to me and we shook hands and then they left."

"What did you do?"

"I stood there and looked around. The restaurant was empty. Eerily quiet, like a tomb. After a few minutes, I shook my head, to clear it, I guess. Then I left."

"You didn't go to your office?"

"No.

"You didn't go anywhere else in the restaurant?"

"No."

"Did you leave by the front entrance again?"

"Yes."

"The 'Closed' sign was still there?"

"Yes."

"Did you go back to the restaurant after that day?"

"Yes."

"Why?

"We were closed, but there were still a lot of valuable things in the restaurant. Utensils, pots, pans, tables, chairs, tableware, glassware, and food supplies in the pantry and the freezer. I decided I had to go back and take inventory. I would sell what I could, and donate the rest to homeless shelters or soup kitchens. I intended to use the money from what I sold to pay part of the salaries owed to the staff. That would reduce what I had to pay out of my own funds."

"Did you intend to do this by yourself?"

"No. I knew I could use some help, so I called Ms. Cavanaugh. She had the background to do inventory and place prices on things."

"What day was this?"

"It was two days after she told me the news."

"Did you reach Ms. Cavanaugh?"

"No. She didn't answer her cell phone and didn't respond to the messages I left for her."

"Did you then take inventory by yourself?"

"Yes."

"Where did you start?"

"I started with the food we had on hand. I knew the hard items would keep, so I started in the pantry. The sooner I knew what was there, I would also know what could be preserved for sale and what was likely to spoil and have to be trashed."

"What did you do next?"

"That took me all day, so I left, intending to return the following day."

"Where did you intend to start when you returned?"

"With the items in the freezer."

"What happened when you returned the next day?"

"I arrived to see that police had cordoned off the area in front of the restaurant."

"What did you do then?"

"I walked up to an officer and told him who I was and asked what was going on."

"He told me to wait. He returned with Detective Thornton."

"Then what?"

"Detective Thornton asked if I knew where Ms. Cavanaugh was. I said I had no idea. Then he asked me when I had seen her last. I asked him what was going on. Then he told me they had found her body in the freezer. That she had frozen to death."

"What happened next?"

"I was told I would have to give a statement and account for my whereabouts over the last few days, from the last time I saw Ms. Cavanaugh up to the time I had arrived at the restaurant to find the police there."

"Thank you. Your witness."

* * *

"Mr. Truitt, let's go over your relationship with the victim. You found her because you were looking for a partner, is that correct?"

"Yes."

"When you first met her in person, what was your impression of her?"

"She was professional. Smart. Was experienced in areas I was not, but those were the areas the business needed."

"Did you find her attractive?"

"Attractive?"

"Yes. Did you find her to be good looking?"

"Yes."

"I believe you testified you didn't socialize with her."

"That's correct."

"Isn't it true that you and she were often alone at the restaurant? After closing, for example?"

"Well, yes."

"And at those times, did you and she meet? Say, to talk about how things were going?"

"Yes."

"Let me show you this photo. Can you identify the people shown in the photo?"

PHOTO

"Er... Yes."

"Please tell the court who those people are."

"It's Ms. Cavanaugh and myself."

"Thank you. This will be Commonwealth Exhibit 13 for the record."

"Looking at Exhibit 13, describe what you see."

"We're sitting outside."

"Were you on a picnic?"

"Yes, we were."

"What are each of you holding?"

"Glasses of wine."

"Was this a special occasion? You seem to be toasting each other, or perhaps some event?"

"Well, it wasn't a big deal. We had just finished putting the final touches on our plans for an updated menu for the restaurant. The weather was particularly nice that day and we decided to celebrate."

"Was there anyone with you?"

"No. Well! I mean we had to ask a passer-by to take the picture."

"But other than that, you and Ms. Cavanaugh were together?"

"Yes."

"What does this photo show, to you?"

"I don't follow."

"Come now Mr. Truitt. You and Ms. Cavanaugh were together. Having a picnic with wine. Both of you are smiling, relaxed."

"Yes."

"This was more than a celebration of having made a new menu, wasn't it?"

"I don't know what you mean."

"You said you and she did not socialize. Do you want to change that assertion?"

"No."

"Just sexual partners then?"

"No."

"Mr. Truitt, you're under oath."

"Running the restaurant was demanding. This time, it was struggling with revising the menu. We did that and were both satisfied we had enhanced the main attraction of any restaurant. But this time, we had finished during the day and not late at night as was more usual. And as I said, the weather was great. So, we decided to celebrate by having a picnic. And that's all."

"Were you in love with her?"

"I don't know. Maybe."

"Was she in love with you?"

"I don't know. Maybe."

"You testified you threatened her when you found out she was stealing. Correct?"

"Yes."

"Is it accurate to say you were so angry you could have killed her?"

"Yes, I said that."

"But your anger wasn't just based on her stealing. It went beyond that, didn't it? Your anger was also because of her betrayal of you. She used sex to distract you. To keep you from asking about the books. The finances."

"No."

"When you found out about the gambling and stealing, you also found out that Gotti was feeding her addiction. Correct?"

"Yes."

"You also testified that she told you she had sex with Gotti in order to buy more time to pay back what she owed him."

"Yes."

"How did that make you feel?"

"I don't know."

"It made you more than mad. It made you jealous. You felt like a fool. When she told you, you struck her and then started to tear off her clothes. You basically raped her and then forced her, naked, into the freezer and allowed the door to shut, knowing it could not be opened from the inside because of the broken handle."

"No! That's not true!"

"Her clothes were not found. What did you do with them?"

"I didn't do what you say. I have no idea where her clothes are."

"You were the only one with the key to the padlock on the freezer. You claimed that you left it unlocked by mistake. But in fact, you locked it to keep anyone from accidentally discovering the body. This was to be sure she laid frozen for several days, making it impossible to determine time of death."

"No! No!"

"Detective Thornton told us that the police received an anonymous phone call tipping them off to investigate the restaurant. When they did, they found the freezer open and her body. You then showed up and played the surprised innocent. Isn't that the truth?"

"No! For God's sake, no!"

"You admit only you had keys to the padlock on the freezer and the back door."

"Yes. That's right."

"Then who else could have gotten into the restaurant or the freezer?"

"I told you. I forgot to lock up. The back door was open and the freezer was too!"

"That's convenient. Why, then, did no one discover her body sooner? Are you saying no one on the staff ever entered the freezer?"

"I told you. When I was told we were losing money, I immediately suspected someone on staff was taking our supplies from the freezer and the pantry. So, I padlocked them both. But that one night, I was upset and left both the freezer and the back door unlocked. Anyone could have entered by the back door."

"Like whom?"

"Like Gotti. He followed her. He would know she was in the restaurant. He would seek entry in the back to stay unseen. He could have jimmied the lock, but didn't have to. The door was unlocked."

"Why would he kill her? She owed him a lot of money, but had paid him a lot of money. If she lives, he still has a chance to collect more."

"Objection, Your Honor. Counsel is badgering the witness. Asking him to speculate on another's actions and motives. The witness has no information to provide."

"Sustained. Move along, Ms. Payne. Save it for your summation."

"No further questions."

"Redirect, Your Honor."

"Go ahead, Ms. Lyle."

* * *

"Mr. Truitt, did you forget to lock the back door one night before Ms. Cavanaugh's body was found?"

"Yes."

"On that same night, did you forget to padlock the freezer?"

"I think I said, I saw no reason to do so any longer since the losses were not due to staff, but rather to Ms. Cavanaugh's stealing."

"On any night before she was found, did you have sex with her?"

"No."

"Did you have a fight or argument during which you tore off some or all of her clothes?"

"No."
"Thank you. That will be all."
"Call your next witness, Ms. Lyle."
"Yes, Your Honor. Defense calls Joey Lee."

CHAPTER 7

Witness For The Defense
Joey Lee

"Mr. Lee, you have just sworn to tell the truth. Do you know that if you don't, it's considered perjury? A crime?

"Yes."

"Where do you currently reside?"

"Deerfield Correctional Center."

"A prison?"

"Yes."

"What are you serving time for?"

"Dealing."

"Drugs?"

"Yeah."

"Why are you testifying in this case?"

"I got some information that's relevant."

"What about?"

"Mr. Gotti."

"You know Mr. Gotti?"

"Yeah. I know him."

"How?"

"You might say we run in the same circles."

"Including prison?"

"Yeah!"

"Which one?"

"Most recently, it was the Loudoun County Adult Detention

Center."

"You and Mr. Gotti were incarcerated there?"

"Yeah."

"What were the circumstances?"

"I was being held awaiting transfer to Deerfield. Gotti had just been arrested for the murder of some chick."

"Did this 'chick' have a name?"

"Yeah. He called her Candy. Candy Cavanaugh.'"

"He talked to you about his arrest?"

"Yeah."

"Why?"

"Gotti's a bragger. He likes to brag about himself."

"What did he brag about to you when you were at the detention center?"

"He said he was arrested for murder, but he wasn't worried."

"Why?"

"He said he'd beat the rap."

"Did he tell you why?"

"Yes. He said he had friends in high places."

"Did he say who these friends were?"

"Not exactly. He hinted at it being someone that got him off another time."

"What else did you talk about?"

"He gave me a run down on the victim."

"What did he tell you about her?"

"Well, he starts off by saying he had a real live one on his hands. Addicted to gambling. Big time! Six figures. He told me she had borrowed a lot, but paid it back at first. He also said she was hot and he took some payments other than cash."

"Did he say what those were?"

"He didn't have to. I knew. He thinks he's a Casanova.

"For the record! You mean sex?"

"Yeah!"

"Go on."

"Well, he said things began to change. She was falling behind more and more. He learned she had been taking money from a partnership she was in. He also learned that she had just about tapped that source out. That concerned him. He didn't want it getting around that some chick was into him big time and that all he was likely to get was laid. He said he could get laid anytime he wanted and didn't need this chick for that—not when she owed him big bucks."

"Go on. What else did he tell you?"

"He also said that he overheard her arguing with her partner. He had obviously learned about her using the company funds to gamble with. They were yelling at each other. It was easy for him to overhear. And he heard something bad."

"What was that?"

"Her partner wanted her to go to the police about Gotti's loans. He argued if she threatened Gotti she was going to turn him in, he'd agree to give some of the money back."

"Did you hear what she responded?"

"Yeah. She was scared. She said Gotti would kill her if he thought she might turn him in."

"Then what did he tell you?"

"I first asked him if he overheard anything more."

"He said he'd heard enough."

"What did he mean by that?"

"Objection, Your Honor. Calls for speculation by the witness."

"Your Honor, may we approach?"

"Yes, Counsel, come forward."

"Your Honor, the witness will testify that Mr. Gotti told him what he meant when he said he had heard enough."

"Very well, Ms. Lyle. Your witness may answer. And Ms. Payne, if I hear anything improper, I will strike it from the record and tell the jury to disregard. Let's proceed."

"Thank you, Your Honor."

"Go ahead, Mr. Lee. You can respond and I'll rule after I hear what you have to say."

"What's the question again?"

"You were asked what Mr. Gotti meant when he told you he had heard enough of what was said at the end of the argument between the two, Ms. Cavanaugh and her partner."

"Oh, yeah! Gotti said that it didn't make any difference now whether the lady overcame her fears. The fact that they were even considering going to the cops sealed her fate. He said he wouldn't stand for being stiffed and then being threatened with being turned in. Bad for business, he said. Emphasized it would be, and I quote, 'very bad.'"

"What else did he tell you?"

"I asked him what he planned to do."

"What did he tell you?"

"He said he already did what he had to do. I looked at him and he began to smile. I said, 'You mean…' and he said, 'Yeah! I frosted her.' I asked what he meant by 'frosted,' and he said, 'Frosted! Like 'ice cubes.'' I asked how. He asked me, 'Where do you get ice cubes?' I said, 'In the freezer.' He said, 'You aren't as dumb as you look.' But then I asked where he was gonna find a freezer big enough, and he said it was no problem, that the victim would provide her own ice coffin."

"Did he tell you anything else?"

"Yeah! I asked him who busted him. He said it was Detective Thornton. He knew I'd know who that was. And I did. We were eventually put in separate cells because I was going to move while Gotti was staying put. When I got to my cell, I tried to get in contact with Thornton."

"Why?"

"I thought if I gave him what Gotti told me, I could bargain for some considerations. Get paroled. Shorter sentence. Minimum-security prison."

"Did you contact Detective Thornton?"

"Yes."

"What happened?"

"He listened."

"That all?"

"Yes."

"He didn't make a deal with you, then?"

"No."

"How did you come about testifying today?"

"I learned the charges against Gotti were dropped and this chick's partner was indicted instead. I got the information that he hired you to defend him. I called you. Told you what I just testified to here. You took it under consideration and then contacted me and said you wanted to meet and go over my story. You told me you needed to be sure I wasn't lying to get a deal for myself. We met. And here I am."

"You affirm that what you testified to just now is what Gotti told you of his own accord?"

"Yeah. I got no way to force anything out of guys like Gotti. He's the strong-arm type. Not me."

"Are you afraid he'll come after you, now that you've testified as you have?"

"It's a risk, yeah. But, that risk is gone if he goes down for this chick's death."

"And if he doesn't, what then?"

"It could get hairy. But, if he doesn't go down, he'd be pretty dumb to come after me. It would just prove what I just told you all is true."

"Still risky though, no?"

"Still risky. But my life is full of risks."

"Thank you, Mr. Lee. Your witness."

* * *

"Mr. Lee, you remember me?"

"Sure! You prosecuted me for some alleged crimes."

"Alleged, you say. Have you been convicted of larceny?"

"Yes. Petty larceny, mind you."

"Passing bad checks?"

"Yes."

"Car theft?"

"Yes."

"Fencing stolen goods?"

"Yes."

"Now drugs?"

"Hey! It was marijuana. Selling it is now legal in a lot of states."

"But not here?"

"Yeah! You'se guys should catch up. It's the twenty-first century already!"

"Your record covers a lot of years, doesn't it?"

"Yeah, but most of those was done in another state. Not here."

"That's supposed to make a difference?"

"Does to me."

"Of course, it would. Why should we believe anything you say, Mr. Lee?"

"Because it's the truth."

"Really?"

"Yeah! I have no reason to lie."

"Really?"

"Yeah! It's not like I told you guys so I could get a reduced sentence, or even parole."

"You want us to believe you're here out of the goodness of your heart?"

"No! That does it! I'll tell you why I'm here."

"Please do. We're all ears, Mr. Lee."

"I would have thought twice about helping out the defense. Like I said, I recognize the risk coming down on a guy like Gotti. But I decided to take the risk because of that Detective Thornton."

"Detective Thornton? Really? Whatever for?"

"I called in good faith to provide some information he could have used. He ignored me. I know he doesn't like me and thinks I'm a two-bit crook. Not worthy of his precious time. But that's arrogant and wrong. You're a prosecutor. You know damn well the cops get a lot of info from people like me. People with records. Usually, they squeeze it out of us by hassling us. Here, I offer info for free and I'm told to pound sand. I says to myself, okay, Mr. High and Mighty doesn't need my help. But, the defense does. So, I call and arrange to tell what I know to Ms. Lyle and her team."

"You did this to help the defendant with his alibis?"

"Yeah!"

"That may or may not be true, Mr. Lee. But that's not the only reason is it, if it really is one?"

"Wadda you mean?"

"I mean you're being paid by counsel or by her client, aren't you?"

"Well? So what?"

"You want this court to believe your testimony when it's been bought and paid for?"

"Hey! You'se guys use expert witnesses all the time. And you pay them—a lot. Paying for testimony is part of the system."

"You're not an expert in anything are you, Mr. Lee?"

"No! I'm no Einstein, if that's what you mean. But I am an expert in one area."

"Oh! And in what area would that be?"

"I know Gotti and his kind. I know when he's on the level because he likes to brag and be the big boss. That's why I know he was telling it like it was with the icing of this chick. I tried to give that to the police. But they couldn't be bothered. So, I took what I knew elsewhere."

"How much have you been paid?"

"Twenty-five Gs."

"Twenty-five thousand dollars. That's a good price for a few hours of telling a story. And it is a story, Mr. Lee, isn't it? None of what you testified to today is true, is it?"

"On my word!"

"On your word? You conned defense counsel and the defendant. You saw them as easy marks. The defendant needed something—someone—to support his claim of innocence. Defense counsel likes to win cases. It bolsters their reputation and draws in more clients and more fees. Your story has plausibility. They buy into what you say and go so far as to pay you to provide your fairytale.

"At the same time, you get revenge on Detective Thornton for dismissing your fiction. Like he testified, he was aware you were a small-time hood. His experience told him not to waste time talking to you. And you used his sound judgment as the reason you went to defense counsel and made your deal."

"Not true!"

"I have no further questions."

"Any redirect, Ms. Lyle?"

* * *

"Yes, Your Honor. Just one question. Mr. Lee, you're under oath. You know the penalties for perjury?"

"Yes."

"If you're lying, and you were tried and convicted, the sentence would be what?"

"I don't follow."

"Your sentence would be for a much longer time than you have previously served. Is that correct?"

"Yes."

"And you just ratted on one who has ties to organized crime?"

"Yeah, I guess so."

"Are you aware that if you were convicted of perjury, you would be sent to a maximum-security prison?"

"I guess so."

"And in those prisons, do those with ties to organized crime have connections with the inmates?"

"Yes."

"The twenty-five thousand dollars you were paid wouldn't be of much use to you under those conditions, would it?"

"No."

"I have no further questions."

CHAPTER 8

Witness For The Defense
Brian Grant

"Please state your name and occupation."

"My name is Brian Grant. I am a professor at the Criminal Justice College in Manassas, Virginia. Before I took my present position, I was a detective for ten years with the homicide squad for the New York City Police Force, working in its organized crime division.

"I decided to teach so that I would have time for research and to study organized crime. I have written and published articles on organized crime. I have been called as an expert witness in cases in which members, believed to be part of organized crime units, were on trial. My testimony was often a deciding factor in the verdicts rendered by the juries sitting in those cases."

"What is the purpose of your testimony in this case?"

"I was hired by your firm, Ms. Lyle, to provide my opinion on what the circumstances surrounding the death of Ms. Candice Cavanaugh show in relation to whether or not organized crime was involved."

"Would you agree that organized crime has many manifestations?"

"Yes. The paradox is that there is a lot of information about organized crime, including who is part of it in any given city, town, or district. Despite this, organized crime may be controlled. But it cannot be eliminated. At least not permanently."

"Does your work concentrate on particular areas or is it more general in approach?"

"I cover as many aspects of organized crime as time and resources permit. For example, loan-sharking, bookmaking, extortion, obstruction of justice. But my focus in these areas has a special concentration on the use of violence and murder in such crimes."

"Can you elaborate on what you just said?"

"Yes, of course. My research and studies have shown that there is a pattern that emerges that demonstrates when violence and murder will be used by typical organized crime enterprises."

"Please explain."

"The public's perception from television and movies is that organized crime almost always means someone or other will be murdered or suffer violent attacks. That is not the case. While there's no hesitancy to resort to such methods, the pattern shows that often, other less- deadly means are preferred. To get the message across, if you will."

"Does that mean that when there is a murder, there are usually circumstances common to its use?"

"Yes. That's correct."

"Can you list some of those circumstances?"

"Yes. If someone within the mob is suspected of being a 'snitch.' If some other mob boss is trying to horn in on the territory of another equally strong boss. If loan-sharking is involved, murder is usually a last resort."

"Why is that?"

"Well, as earlier testimony has shown, if the debtor is killed, it's a certainty that no more money will be coming back."

"Using that logic, why would anyone owing the mob be killed?"

"Organized crime is run like a business in a lot of ways. One principal is to cut your losses. Say someone owes the mob $25,000 or more and has been consistently late in paying his installments or paying less than what was agreed would be the minimum. Say this has been going on for weeks or months."

"How does the length of the delinquency factor in?"

"I'll get to that in a minute. As I was saying, if he's been late and/or short for some time, first, he's warned. Then threatened. Then roughed up. Having gotten the message, he comes up with some payment. But if he's still short, his next visit is likely to be his last. The mob understands the business principle of cutting your losses.

"That is, there are any number of others in debt to the loan shark. Let's say ten others. It's better to lose one deadbeat to send the message to the other ten that they had better pay up than keep the delinquent alive and give him more time to pay. Moreover, given the exorbitant interest charged, the timing for the killing can be set so that the mob still makes plenty based on what the deadbeat has been able to repay up until he's outed."

"The timing?"

"The timing of the hit depends on several factors. Is the delinquent known to others with outstanding loans? How big was the original loan amount? How big is the delinquency? What are the chances that others, if they don't already know about the delinquency, will find out about it? Are there any other circumstances about the delinquent or handling of the loan that might embarrass the loan shark? Make him look bad? Make him look like a patsy? Depending on what the combination of such circumstances are, they can dictate that the coup de gras has to be delivered after only several weeks have passed or several months."

"And the hit itself? What can you tell us about that?"

"It is usually gruesome in some way. The object is to scare others not only for their lives, but for being tortured before killed. Of being killed in some horrible way. Being burned to death. Being buried alive. Being cut to pieces while tied up. Being drowned. Or being 'iced,' as in the case of Ms. Cavanaugh.

"Most of us are afraid of dying. But there's an inherent fear of dying a horrible death, full of pain and ugliness before the end. Such killings send the ultimate message. If you don't want to suffer the same or similar gruesome fate, pay up on time and in full, or else."

"What have you examined in preparation for your testimony today?"

"I have reviewed Detective Thornton's investigative reports. I reviewed the autopsy report on Ms. Cavanaugh. I visited the scene of the crime, the freezer, the restaurant area, kitchen and offices, and photographs of the decedent's body where it was found. In the presence of his counsel, I interviewed Mr. Truitt. I also visited some of the casinos frequented by Ms. Cavanaugh."

"What conclusions did you reach?"

"Based upon my review of the foregoing, and my background on organized crime, I would conclude that Ms. Cavanaugh's murder was a mob hit."

"Can you elaborate?"

"Yes. It's been established that Ms. Cavanaugh was addicted to gambling. That she bet in large amounts. Over time she suffered losses in equally large amounts. She had a history of seeking to cover her losses by asking her well-off family to cover her losses. But after going to that well so many times, that source dried up. She did not make the kind of money to cover her losses. She knew she could not obtain financing from any of the standard sources. Her only option was to go to someone like Ray Gotti. It's unclear if she knew how to contact someone like him.

"Indeed, I was at first puzzled about how she would have contacted him. My visits to the casinos solved that. When shown pictures of Ms. Cavanaugh and Mr. Gotti, several of the staff recalled seeing them together. They were usually seen at the bars, talking. Occasionally, he would join her at one of the tables where she was gambling. A couple of people saw him take what most would call 'liberties' with her, such as touching her. They said she looked as if she didn't like it, but tolerated it. Gotti, being a mobster, knew he could get away with such things.

"Ultimately, she started to lose more than she won. More and more, she became late in her payments. Having nowhere to turn, and, being in charge of the restaurant's finances, with a partner she knew did not check the books, using the partnership's money was the only thing she could do. Her decision was made easier after she was physically abused for missing yet more repayment dates.

"At some point, Gotti learned where she was getting the money. That was fine until he realized the restaurant was facing bankruptcy and she wouldn't be able to make any more payments. At that point, she became a liability—a liability that grew worse when he overheard she might go to the police.

"Then, the way she was murdered has all the earmarks of a mob hit. Preventing a determination of her time of death. The absence of relevant DNA at the site. Leaving the body unclothed and none of her clothing located in the restaurant. All of these indicate a thoroughly planned murder indicative of the involvement of, and execution by, organized crime, to which she was heavily in debt; heavily delinquent with her only source of money now gone.

"These factors also dispute the theory that her murder was committed in the heat of passion by someone victimized by her betrayal, deceit, and selfishness."

"In your opinion, did Mr. Truitt commit this crime?"

"No."

"In your opinion, is Mr. Lee telling the truth about what Mr. Gotti told him about Ms. Cavanaugh's murder and his boasting that he had connections that meant he wouldn't stand trial for her murder?"

"In my opinion, yes."

"Why?"

"Those in organized crime develop big egos. Look at me, I'm getting rich! People are scared of me. I'm living the high life! Big cars! Fancy duds! Broads! Big house with a swimming pool. Membership in exclusive clubs. Hobnob with some politicos! That's not enough, though. When you have the chance, you brag about your latest caper.

Especially when you know, even though you are fingered, you won't be held responsible."

"Can you elaborate on your last comment? You refer to not being held responsible?"

"Yes. My work, background, research, and studies unfortunately establish that often, organized crime survives and prospers due to the corruption of law enforcement. Fortunately, it doesn't happen or succeed that often. But it cannot be denied that it does succeed at times."

"In your opinion, do you think corruption was involved in this case?"

"In my opinion, it's possible, but not clear."

"Why?"

"Detective Thornton has been investigated for allegedly tampering with evidence that disappeared in a case against Gotti. Because of the lack of evidence, Gotti walked. To avoid any appearance of collusion, it would have been best if Detective Thornton had not been assigned to this case. Or when assigned, would have recused himself."

"Are you saying you suspect that when Gotti told Mr. Lee he had connections in this case that would see to it that he wasn't tried for Ms. Cavanaugh's murder, he was referring to Detective Thornton?"

"I'm saying, it comes down to what one believes after hearing all the testimony and determining what makes most sense.

What is most credible? In that context, Mr. Lee's testimony is complicating the situation. Does that mean I believe Mr. Lee was referring to Detective Thornton? No! Most certainly not! But I am saying that had Detective Thornton not taken this case, the complication of his possible involvement with Gotti wouldn't exist, in my opinion."

"Mr. Grant, what have you been paid to render your expert opinion in this case?"

"Normally, my rate is $500 an hour to provide expert testimony. I spent forty hours preparing, so the total fee is $20,000. But, knowing the financial circumstances the defendant is in, along with other factors, I agreed to take half that amount."

"Thank you. That's all I have."

"You're up, Ms. Payne."

* * *

"Thank you, Your Honor."

"Mr. Grant, would you say it was possible that your extensive dealings in the doings of organized crime has ever shaded your judgment?"

"Do you mean is my judgment dominated or fixated such that whenever there are elements of organized crime found in my investigations, I will always conclude that organized crime was involved or responsible?"

"Yes, that provides an excellent understanding of my point."

"First, I provide testimony for both prosecution and defense. That helps me keep my balance. But I think your question is fair because one can be influenced by repeated exposure to similar facts and circumstances. Particularly when they often contain patterns of conduct that are vicious and disgusting."

"Then let me ask you this. In this case, you have circumstances, not necessarily facts, that include the following: Detective Thornton and Gotti have a prior history. One in which it was perhaps believed, but never proven, that Detective Thornton was responsible for Gotti getting off by tampering with evidence. Indeed, no disciplinary action of any kind was taken. Then there's Mr. Lee's allegations that Gotti told him he had connections that ensured him he would not be tried for Ms. Cavanaugh's murder.

"You have asserted that Detective Thornton should have recused himself from the investigation into her death. But he didn't. Now let me pause here and ask you this: When did you arrive at the conclusion that Detective Thornton should have recused himself? Was it before or after you knew Gotti was originally charged? Or was it after you learned what Mr. Lee would testify to?"

"It was after I learned that Detective Thornton dropped his charges against Gotti and charged Mr. Truitt."

"Why then?"

"I knew of his prior involvement with Gotti and what had happened back then. Sure, it was never proven that Thornton did anything to help Gotti that time. But, in my view, his involvement in another case in which Gotti was a central figure and certainly a suspect, would create the appearance of impropriety. I have nothing against the detective. I thought it was for his own good and for making a case against whomever committed the crime."

"In your experience, have you ever had a case in which the elements of the crime indicated that organized crime was involved, only to find out that it was not?"

"That's very unusual."

"Unusual, but not impossible?"

"Yes."

"Have you ever worked on a case in which that actually happened?"

"Only one time."

"Tell us the circumstances."

"It was a murder case. The method of killing. The victim had some dealings with the mob. Other factors indicated that it was a mob hit."

"But it turned out not to be?"

"Correct."

"What was it, then?"

"It was made to look like a mob hit to throw suspicion off the real perpetrator."

"Was the real perpetrator apprehended and tried?"

"Yes."

"Was this after or before the organized crime figure was arrested and tried?"

"It was after he was arrested and on trial when new evidence came to light that indicated he could not have committed the crime."

"Mr. Grant, let me give you this scenario in this case. And you provide your opinion or comments afterward."

"Okay."

"The defendant in this case suffered a huge financial loss and his business. His partner in whom he had, until then, complete and absolute trust, stole from him and betrayed him. He learns all this happened because of her gambling addiction. He learns that Mr. Gotti was the one she was involved with to get the money to keep gambling. Then he learns she used the partnership's funds to pay Gotti back.

"The defendant also knew that Ms. Cavanaugh was afraid of Gotti and had been roughed up and even forced to have sex with him. His suggestion that she go to the authorities on the possibility that turning Gotti in could lead to recouping some of the partnership's money is turned down because Ms. Cavanaugh feared for her life if she did so.

"And for the defendant, that's the last straw. She ruined him and his business, then wouldn't do anything to at least try to get back some of the money. She wouldn't do it because she was afraid Gotti would kill her or have her killed. His anger grows and he snaps. Here she is, sitting quietly at her desk in the restaurant that wouldn't be opening again. Here she is, sitting there after admitting she had sex with Gotti to feed her addiction. He sees the opportunity.

The funds from the Buy-Sell agreement will allow him to start over. But he gets those funds only if she is dead. He decides she deserves to die. But he knows the insurance company won't pay if he is found to have caused her death. To throw off suspicion, he decides to make it look like a mob hit. He strips her and shoves her into the freezer that cannot be opened from the inside. Then he waits. Several days later, she is discovered. By then, no DNA, other than her own. No time of death. He tells the police he saw Gotti hanging around. The conclusion? Gotti murdered her to send a message to others not to cheat on the mob."

"Clever, Ms. Payne. But it's all based on supposition. As I already testified, in my opinion the circumstances of the murder indicate it was carefully planned and executed like so many other mob murders that I've investigated. That excludes the possibility in my opinion that she was murdered in a heat of passion. Indeed, the scene you describe is a prime example of a cold and calculated execution."

"Are you saying the defendant is not capable of cold calculation?"

"He may well be, but not in this case. The murder was too brutal. She suffered humiliation before she was killed. All the circumstances indicate that she was killed by someone used to cold-blooded killing. In this case, there is a cold-blooded killer involved. Ray Gotti. He had motive, opportunity, and acquired the means by using the restaurant's freezer."

"You cannot say that the defendant did not have a similar motive. Recovery of a large sum of money. Opportunity. At the restaurant. And unrestricted access to the freezer."

"No. I cannot."

"I have no further questions."

"Ms. Lyle, any redirect?"

"Yes, Your Honor."

* * *

"Mr. Grant, has the line of questioning the prosecution just conducted change your opinion that Ms. Cavanaugh was murdered in gangland style like many other murders committed by organized crimes?"

"No."

"And the only organized crime figure known to be involved with Ms. Cavanaugh was Ray Gotti."

"That's my understanding."

"In your opinion, who killed Ms. Cavanaugh?"

"It was Gotti."

"He didn't contract the hit?"

"No. Gotti's not big enough to hire hit men. He would do the job himself."

"Thank you. No further questions."

* * *

"That's enough for today. Tomorrow, counsel will give their closing statements and I will give my instructions to the jury. Thereafter, the jury may retire for its deliberations. Court is adjourned."

CHAPTER 9

Closing Arguments
Jury Instructions

"The court is now in session. Counsel will now present their closing arguments. Ms. Payne, you may begin."

"Thank you, Your Honor. Ladies and gentlemen of the jury, this case is full of tragedies. The first, of course, is that a talented, attractive, and successful woman, Candice Cavanaugh, suffered from a terrible addiction. Unable to control her addiction, and needing to feed it, she got caught up in the whirlpool that is the underworld. When she couldn't handle the swirling vortex of borrowing, repaying, and defaulting, she suffered the consequences of threats and physical abuse.

"With no place to turn, she stole from her partner. Betrayed his trust. Brought ruin to their joint enterprise for which she paid the ultimate price—her life. She was brutally and callously murdered.

"Then there is the defendant's tragedy. He worked long and hard to create the business he wanted. He found a partner with the skills and knowledge he needed to ensure the success of that business. But that partner betrayed him and ruined his business. One can only imagine his emotions when the truth was finally revealed.

"Then there's another tragedy. It's not center stage. But it is there in the wings. It's Detective Keith Thornton. His honor and career have been attacked. Testimony attempts to link him to aiding and abetting a mob figure, Ray Gotti. Helping him get off for his alleged involvement with the murder of Ms. Cavanaugh.

"In your deliberations, you need to keep these tragedies in perspective. They should not influence your consideration of the facts that have been presented in trial. Those facts show that the defendant was irate when he found out about his partner's betrayal. He admitted he was angry enough to kill her for her betrayal, and in fact threatened to do so. Bringing financial ruin on a business is a common motive for murder. But, that was not the only factor.

"You have heard testimony that the defendant's efforts failed to persuade Ms. Cavanaugh to go to the police about Gotti's loan sharking in the hopes of recouping some of the money she paid him with the partnership's funds. Then, there is the Buy-Sell agreement and the insurance payout that would provide funds to rescue the business. But, the defendant would not receive that payout unless Ms. Cavanaugh was dead.

"The defendant was by this time well aware of Gotti's involvement in causing the disaster that had befallen him. It was no big leap to put two and two together. Ms. Cavanaugh's refusal to go to the police about Gotti ended any compassion the defendant may have had for her addiction. Not only was she responsible for the financial disaster, she refused to make the effort to reduce its effects. She told him she refused out of fear for her life. That Gotti would kill her.

"The solution to the defendant's financial problems dawned on him. To realize the proceeds from the Buy-Sell agreement, Ms. Cavanaugh had to die. To ensure the clause in the insurance contract that forfeited the payout could not be invoked, there could be no question raised that he might be involved in her death. Solution? Make her murder look like a mob hit, pointing the finger directly at Gotti as the murderer.

"The defendant's plan worked perfectly at first. Gotti was charged for her murder. But further investigation led to a different conclusion. And that conclusion was that the defendant had the motive, the opportunity, and the means to kill Ms. Cavanaugh. The charges were dropped against Gotti and Mr. Truitt was charged with her murder.

"The defendant denies he killed Ms. Cavanaugh. You must consider that denial in proper context. It's obvious that anyone would deny guilt for murdering someone. But then there's the testimony of Mr. Lee. That Gotti bragged he had made the hit. Was unconcerned because he had connections. The implication being that because Detective Thornton was the investigating officer and was alleged to have aided Gotti before, Gotti would beat the rap. But think! There is no corroborative evidence to support Mr. Lee's testimony. Mr. Lee has a criminal record. He admits he was paid for his testimony."

"Then, there's the testimony of Mr. Grant. Based on his experience and research of organized crime, in his opinion the murder was typical of a mob hit. That the means and circumstances of the killing indicated to him that the killing could not have been done in the heat of passion. He concludes the defendant could not have done the killing, leaving Mr. Gotti as the murderer.

"Makes sense. But wait! In considering Mr. Grant's testimony, keep the following in mind: First, it's opinion only. Not fact. Second, that the defendant could only have committed the murder in the heat of passion is supposition.

"Had Ms. Cavanaugh been killed shortly after the defendant discovered her betrayal, the theory she was killed in the heat of passion requires consideration. But, Ms. Cavanaugh was killed well after the defendant's discovery of her betrayal. Knowing he needed Ms. Cavanaugh dead to get the insurance, and knowing chances were good that blame would fall on Gotti, his indictment would insure the defendant would get the insurance. In short, the defendant was in full control and carried out his plans in cold blood.

"The correct verdict in this sea of tragedies is to find the defendant guilty for the murder of Candice Cavanaugh. Thank you."

"Ms. Lyle?"

* * *

"Thank you, Your Honor. Ladies and gentlemen, you will be receiving instructions from the court on the law and the burden of proof. Pay particular attention to the court's instructions on the burden of proof the prosecution must bear. He will instruct you that the Commonwealth must prove beyond a reasonable doubt that the defendant committed this crime. That beyond a reasonable doubt, he intended to and did kill Ms. Cavanaugh. That beyond a reasonable doubt, he killed her in a most brutal and indecent manner. That beyond a reasonable doubt, he was calculatingly ruthless, making it look like a mob hit. That beyond a reasonable doubt, he executed the murder so that the time of death could not be determined. That no incriminating DNA would be found.

"The defense, the defendant, has no burden of proof. The defendant is innocent until proven guilty beyond a reasonable doubt. That verdict must be unanimous. All of you, each one of you, must agree that there is no reasonable doubt in any of your minds that the defendant intended to, and did in fact, murder Ms. Cavanaugh in a most foul manner.

"But, let's look at the evidence. The defendant took the stand in his own defense. He admitted he was more than just angry. He was angry enough to want to kill her. Ask yourself! How would you react given the shock of first learning that your business was out of money? And then, that your partner was the cause because of an addiction she never disclosed? Nor for which she ever sought help? Yet, when asked directly if he did kill Ms. Cavanaugh, he answers with one word: 'No.' He doesn't make excuses. He doesn't go into a long speech. He just says, 'No. I didn't do it.'"

"Ms. Cavanaugh's addiction led her to become involved with a small-time hood named Ray Gotti. As explained by Mr. Grant, an expert on organized crime, Ms. Cavanaugh's murder had all the earmarks of a mob hit. It was purposefully gruesome and grotesque because a message had to be sent to others that owed the mob money: 'You don't pay up and something bad, very bad, will happen to you.'

"You have heard evidence that Ms. Cavanaugh had been threatened by Mr. Gotti. That she was physically abused by him when she didn't pay on time or in full. Out of fear and desperation, she even consented to have sex with him. Then Gotti overheard her being urged to go to the police. You heard the testimony that she refused out of fear for her life if she did. She was afraid that Gotti would kill her. At this point, Gotti, a known racketeer, could not afford to take any chances. He could not risk her changing her mind or succumbing to Mr. Truitt's pleas that she do so.

"And take note here. There is no evidence that Ms. Cavanaugh was at any time afraid of Mr. Truitt. Not even after he threatened to kill her.

"Next, let's look at the testimony of Joey Lee. Admittedly, he's a small-time hoodlum. He was paid for his testimony and you can take that into account. When you do, keep these things in mind: Lee knows if it is proven that he is lying to get his payment, he would be convicted not only of perjury, but also obstruction of justice. These are big-time offenses, and on conviction, he would be incarcerated in a high-security prison. The money he was paid would do him no good at that point, just like he said when he testified.

"And consider, that what he testified Gotti told him was based on Gotti's boast that he knew he wouldn't serve any time because of his connections. Can it be proven that he was referring to Detective Thornton? Consider this! While working undercover, Thornton admitted he had developed a relationship with Gotti. That to be effective, he had to get Gotti to trust him and that Gotti did trust him.

And consider, that Gotti got off another time because evidence was lost. The circumstances warranted an investigation into whether the detective involved in that case, Detective Thornton, tampered with the evidence. He was cleared. But, why? Because he wasn't responsible for losing the evidence, or because there wasn't sufficient proof he did?

"In fairness, you must accept the fact that Detective Thornton was not shown to be responsible for Gotti's walking on those other charges. But, as Mr. Grant testified, given that past, it would have been best had the detective recused himself from this investigation of Ms. Cavanaugh's murder as soon as he learned that Gotti was involved. Not only did he fail to do that, but his first conclusion 'based on his experience' was that her murder was a mob hit and that Gotti was responsible.

"Then he changes his mind. Why? Because Mr. Truitt threatened her. Because he would benefit from the Buy-Sell agreement's insurance payment. Certainly, Mr. Truitt had motives: anger and reward. But as we all know, the reward is forfeit if he was responsible for his partner's death.

"Mr. Truitt is a restauranteur, a chef. He has no criminal record of any kind. Ever. But, according to the Commonwealth attorney's theory, he all of a sudden developed the murdering talent of the mob. Not only did he execute the victim in gang-land style, he cleaned up after the killing so that no direct evidence of his involvement could be found.

"He somehow, out-of-nowhere, knew that a frozen corpse would provide little DNA other than that of the victim's. And freezing would prevent a determination of the time of death. He all-of-a-sudden knew to get rid of her clothing to prevent finding any DNA on it. The fact that his fingerprints were found is not incriminating. It's exculpatory. Why? Because if his fingerprints weren't found in his restaurant it would be incriminating. It would indicate he wiped the place down.

"No, ladies and gentlemen of the jury. The prosecution has failed to prove beyond a reasonable doubt that the defendant murdered Ms. Cavanaugh. Therefore, you must return a verdict of 'not guilty' on all counts. Thank you."

* * *

"Your Honor?"

"Yes, Ms. Payne?"

"A short rebuttal?"

"It's the prosecution's right. Go ahead."

"Thank you. Ladies and gentlemen, just a few facts to keep in mind. First, that it might have been a better course had Detective Thornton recused himself as Mr. Grant suggests, avoiding the appearance of impropriety is not a factor on which your decision can be based. It's a supposition and not fact. It does not prove that Detective Thornton changed his determination of who was responsible for Ms. Cavanaugh's murder because of his previous contacts with Mr. Gotti. Second, if done in the heat of passion, the defendant would not have thought about the forfeiture clause in the Buy-Sell agreement's insurance policy. And thirdly, surely, when he first found out about the victim's treachery, any harmful actions he would have taken at that time would result from his anger, resentment, and thirst for revenge. This raises a question whether so much time had passed that the heat of passion had cooled.

"But what if his passion was rekindled? How? Ms. Cavanaugh

refuses to go to the police about Gotti. She destroyed his hope of recouping any of his financial loss. Then, he remembers the insurance clause. With Gotti taking the fall, his problems are solved. Yet, she refuses to help. His anger is rekindled. But now, it's cold and calculating. Because he knows when he kills Ms. Cavanaugh he must implicate Gotti.

"The defendant is not a hardened criminal. But such terrible circumstances as he faced could make anyone a murderer. And a clever one at that. Thank you."

"Thank you, Ms. Payne. The court will stand in recess until 2:00 p.m. When we reconvene, I will give the jury its instructions."

* * *

"Members of the Jury, it is my duty as the court to instruct you about the law and your duties as jurors. So please pay close attention.

"This is a criminal case commenced by the Commonwealth against the Defendant, Carl Truitt. He has been charged with murder in the first degree.

"Concerning burden of proof and the presumption of innocence, the Defendant has pleaded 'not guilty' and is presumed to be innocent. The Commonwealth has the burden of proving the guilt of the defendant Carl Truitt beyond a reasonable doubt. A reasonable doubt is a doubt based upon reason and common sense—the kind of doubt that would make a reasonable person hesitate to act in the graver and more important affairs of life.

"Murder in the first degree requires that the killing be shown to be intentional. The defendant is guilty of murder in the first degree only if it is found that he intentionally caused the death of the victim, Ms. Candice Cavanaugh. Stated perhaps more clearly, for you to find the defendant guilty of murder in the first degree, you all must find that the following two elements have been established beyond a reasonable doubt. First, the defendant caused Ms. Cavanaugh's death. Second, the defendant acted intentionally.

"To prove that the defendant 'caused' Ms. Cavanaugh's death, the Commonwealth must establish that she would not have died but for the defendant's conduct.

'Intentionally' means that it was the defendant's conscious objective or purpose to cause the victim's death.

"If, after considering all the evidence, you find that the Commonwealth has established beyond a reasonable doubt that the defendant acted in such a manner as to satisfy all the elements that I have just stated, on or about the date and at the place stated in the indictment, you should find the defendant guilty of murder in the first degree. If you find that the Commonwealth has not proven every element of the offense beyond a reasonable doubt, then you must find the defendant not guilty of murder in the first degree.

"You may also consider that there may be a lesser included offense, namely, manslaughter. If you conclude beyond a reasonable doubt that the defendant intentionally caused the death of Ms. Cavanaugh, you should next consider whether he did so while under the influence of extreme emotional distress. The fact that the defendant intentionally caused the death of another person while under the influence of extreme emotional distress is a mitigating circumstance which reduces the crime of murder in the first degree to the crime of manslaughter.

"However, it is the defendant who has the burden of proving, by a preponderance of the evidence, that he acted under the influence of extreme emotional distress. The defendant must also prove, by a preponderance of the evidence, that there is a reasonable explanation or excuse for the existence of the extreme emotional distress. The reasonableness of the explanation or excuse must be determined from the viewpoint of a reasonable person in the defendant's situation under the circumstances as he believed them to be.

"The purpose of the law of the mitigating circumstance of extreme emotional distress is to permit the defendant to show that the intentional killing was caused by a sort of frenzy of mind and that he is, therefore, less culpable for the killing. This mitigating circumstance applies to persons who kill, in part, because of unique factors that cause an emotional explosion or as an extreme reaction to overwhelming stress.

"You should give the words 'extreme emotional distress' their common, everyday meaning. A person under the influence of extreme emotional distress is someone whose feelings were thrown into extraordinary, unusual, or unexpected disorder. Extreme emotional distress is a type of mental or physical feeling of such exceptional stress, excitement, or disturbance as to produce a frenzy of mind which makes one deaf to the voice of reason. It is a condition or state of mind that can occur spontaneously or it can develop over time.

"In addition to proving that he acted under the influence of extreme emotional distress, the defendant must also prove, by a preponderance of the evidence, that there is a reasonable explanation or excuse for the existence of the extreme emotional distress. That is, you must consider whether a reasonable person in the defendant's position or situation under the circumstances as he believed them to be would have suffered from extreme emotional distress.

"To be a reasonable explanation, the event that triggered the emotional disturbance must be something external from the defendant and cannot be something for which the defendant was responsible, such as involvement in a crime.

"If the defendant intentionally, knowingly, recklessly, or negligently brought about his own mental disturbance, extreme emotional distress is not applicable. Further, if the defendant's mental state was caused by voluntary alcohol or drug use, extreme emotional distress is not applicable.

"Next, you may consider murder in the second degree. If you find the defendant not guilty of murder in the first degree, you must decide if the Commonwealth has proven beyond a reasonable doubt that the defendant committed murder in the second degree. Under our laws, a person is guilty of murder in the second degree when he recklessly causes the death of another person under circumstances which manifest a cruel, wicked, and depraved indifference to human life.

"In other words, to find the defendant guilty of murder in the second degree, you must find that each of the following three elements has been established beyond a reasonable doubt. First, the defendant caused the victim's death. Second, the defendant acted recklessly.

Third, the defendant's recklessness manifested a cruel, wicked, and depraved indifference to human life.

"To prove that the defendant 'caused' Ms. Cavanaugh's death, the Commonwealth must establish that she would not have died but for the defendant's conduct.

'Recklessly' means that the defendant was aware of and consciously disregarded a substantial and unjustifiable risk that Ms. Cavanaugh's death would result from his conduct.

"The Commonwealth must demonstrate that the risk was of such a nature and degree that the defendant's disregard of it was a gross deviation from the standard of conduct that a reasonable person would observe under the same circumstances.

"'Cruel' describes the malicious infliction of physical suffering upon a human being. 'Depraved' describes an indifference for human life. 'Wicked' describes a lack of conscience or morality. If, after considering all the evidence, you find that the Commonwealth has established beyond a reasonable doubt that the defendant acted in such a manner as to satisfy all of the elements that I have just stated, on or about the date and at the place stated in the indictment, you should find the defendant guilty of murder in the second degree.

"If you find that the Commonwealth has not proven every element of the offense beyond a reasonable doubt, then you must find the defendant not guilty of murder in the second degree.

"Now for some general instructions. You alone are the judges of the credibility of the witnesses and the weight to be given to the testimony of each of them. In determining the credit to be given any witness, you should take into account his truthfulness or untruthfulness, his ability and opportunity to observe, his memory, his manner while testifying, any interest, bias, or prejudice he may have and the reasonableness of his testimony considered in light of all the evidence in the case.

"You should consider each opinion received in evidence in this case and give it such weight as you think it deserves. If you should conclude that the reasons given in support of the opinion are not sound or that for any other reason an opinion is not correct, you may disregard that opinion entirely. Despite a witness being qualified as an expert in some subject pertaining to this case does not entitle his testimony to be accepted uncritically.

"The law governing this case is contained in these instructions, and it is your duty to follow the law. You must consider these instructions in their entirety. You must not pick out one instruction or parts of an instruction and disregard others.

"You are the sole judges of the facts in this case. It is your duty to determine the facts from the evidence produced here in court. Your verdict should not be based on speculation, guess, or conjecture. Neither sympathy nor prejudice should influence your verdict. You are to apply the law as stated in these instructions to the facts as you find them, and in this way, decide the case. You must not concern yourself with the consequences of your verdict.

"Your verdict must represent the considered judgment of each juror. In order to return a verdict, it is necessary that each juror agrees. Your verdict must be unanimous. It is your duty to consult with one another and try to reach an agreement. However, you are not required to give up your individual judgment. Each of you must decide the case for yourself, but you must do so only after an impartial consideration of the evidence with your fellow jurors.

"During the course of your deliberations, do not hesitate to re-examine your own view and change your opinion if you are convinced it is erroneous. But do not surrender your honest conviction as to the weight or effect of evidence solely because of the opinion of your fellow jurors. Do not surrender your opinion to reach a verdict. You are the judges—judges of the facts. Your sole interest is to ascertain the truth from the evidence in the case.

"You will now retire to the jury room and select one of you to act as foreperson. That person will preside over your deliberations and will speak for the jury here in court. Verdict forms have been prepared for your convenience. You will take these forms to the jury room. When you have reached unanimous agreement as to your verdict, the foreperson will sign the forms which express your verdict. You will then return all forms of verdict, these instructions, and any exhibits to the courtroom.

"Thank you for your attention. You will need to pick a foreperson who will contact the clerk if there is a need to contact me with questions or for other matters that may arise during your deliberations. You may now retire and start your deliberations. The court stands in recess."

CHAPTER 10

Jury Deliberations

"Ladies and gentlemen, my name is Joseph Michael, the bailiff. As His Honor indicated, I will be your contact should you want to contact the judge or have other questions or needs. To get started, you need to choose a foreperson. To assist you, please pass around this sheet. It briefly identifies each of you by name and provides a brief statement of your backgrounds. The numbers following your names is the number used to identify you during voir dire as Juror 1, Juror 2, and so forth."

Dennis O. Robertson 1
Originally from Fishers Island, New York. Retired military. Among tours of duty were four years in Germany, the Army Staff, and the Office of the Joint Chiefs of Staff. Served in the 77th Infantry Division, the 25th Infantry Division, and the 1st Infantry Division.

Frederick R. Koger 2
Annandale, Virginia. Career federal employee with the U.S. Patent and Trademark Office.

Alex T. Hunt 3
Originally from Milwaukee, Wisconsin. CPA and Certified Financial Planner

Maurice F. McCubbins 4
Originally from Philadelphia, Pennsylvania. Family medicine practice, teaches clinical medicine at Georgetown University Hospital, and serves as Chief of Family Practice, Fairfax County Hospital.

Deborah A. Kay 5
From Bryn Mawr, Pennsylvania, graduate of Vassar College, Poughkeepsie, New York with a degree in child psychology. Now stays at home with six children.

George S. Stevens 6
From North Caldwell, New Jersey. Graduate of the Wharton School of the University of Pennsylvania. Currently Vice President at Oppenheimer & Co.

Marie V. Churchill 7
Originally from Dunmore, Pennsylvania. Resides in Purcellville, Virginia. Graduated from George Mason University. Previously on the Fairfax County School Board and Fairfax County Board of Supervisors. Runs her own government relations and consulting firm.

Janet Y. Toland 8
Originally from Portland, Oregon. Foreign Service Officer having served in Belgium, Greece, Turkey, Argentina, Hong Kong, Mexico, and just returned from her last assignment in the Philippines.

Charles N. Hudgins 9
Originally from Glen Rock, Pennsylvania. Works for

American Airlines as a maintenance instructor and supervisor at Reagan National Airport and investor in Northern Virginia real estate.

Gertrude P. Allan 10
Native of Leesburg, Virginia. Former legal secretary now works for social services.

Mary M. Josephson 11
Graduated from Trinity College, has her Master of Social Work from Boston College and her Ph.D. from Catholic University and currently works for Loudon County Family Service Department.

Michelle J. Lasner 12
Originally from Upper Marlboro, Maryland. Has a degree in Business Administration, Accounting, and Economics from the University of Maryland. Works for software company serving the U.S. House of Representatives.

* * *

"If no one objects, I'll volunteer to be the foreperson. I'm Gertrude Allan; I formerly worked as a legal secretary. The law firm I worked for was basically a trial firm, trying both civil and criminal cases. I'm acquainted with trial practice and thought it may be helpful."

"I'm George Stevens. One question, Ms. Allan. I assume your attorneys only represented the defense in criminal cases. Would that affect your judgement here?"

"Fair question. But the answer is no. There were times I thought the firm's clients in some cases were guilty. But they were entitled to a defense. If I thought I had a bias for the defense, I wouldn't offer to be the foreperson."

"I'm Michelle Lasner, Juror 12. I have no problem with Ms. Allan acting as foreperson. All in favor, raise their hands… It appears you have been selected as foreperson, Ms. Allan."

"Thank you. Let's start, then, to see where each of us stands now. I'll pass around copies of the verdict cards. Write down your current position of 'guilty,' 'guilty of a lesser included offense,' 'not guilty,' or 'undecided.' Of course, do not identify yourself and do not show your card to another juror. Place them face down in front of you on the table. I'll collect them and read the results."

* * *

"I have all the cards now. I'll read each one as I turn them over. Keep in mind that unless this straw poll shows we are unanimous in the verdict, whether 'guilty' or 'not guilty,' I will dispose of the cards and we will need to begin our deliberations.

"Guilty."
"Guilty."
"Undecided."
"Not guilty."
"Undecided."
"Guilty of lesser offense."
"Not guilty."
"Undecided."
"Not Guilty."
"Guilty."
"Undecided."
"Guilty of lesser offense."

"That's three 'guilty,' two 'guilty of lesser offense,' three 'not guilty,' and four 'undecided.' Well, that's a divided vote."

"Ms. Allan, you've seen all the votes. I think you should tell the rest of us how you voted."

"To what purpose, Mr. Hudgins?"

"Knowing how you voted as foreperson and with your legal background and experience, it might be instructive."

"Well, I doubt it, but I voted 'undecided.'"

"Why?"

"I don't wish to be an influence, other than perhaps in this way. I think this is a difficult case with a lot of evidence that goes one way and another. Under such circumstances, I think we need to go over the evidence and discuss how we interpret it and the reasons for those interpretations. Obviously, the evidence is being interpreted differently. Why? Discussion, debate, and analysis is what's needed if we hope to reach a unanimous verdict."

"With a background in psychology, I have to agree. My background is in child psychology, so I'm not claiming any expertise in what we are asked to decide. But, in general, I know that exploring our individual approaches to decision making should provide insights that can be helpful in ultimately pointing to a consensus."

"Thank you, Dr. Kay. Let's begin. Who wants the floor first? Yes, Mr. Dennis Robertson."

"I find Truitt guilty. He lost everything because of Cavanaugh. Someone he trusted. Someone he depended on. And she wouldn't lift a finger to try and get some money back when he asked. If it had been me, I'd want her to pay."

"Are you saying you would have killed her, Mr. Robertson?"

"No, I guess not. But I am saying Truitt killed her."

"Ms. Toland?"

"I vote 'not guilty.' I just can't accept that the defendant who has no criminal record, no history of any kind of violence would so brutally kill someone. Someone he has worked with closely and may have been in love with, although he may not have known that himself."

"That's a leap. There was little or no evidence, was there, that indicated he was in love with the victim?"

"That's correct I believe, Dr. McCubbins. Ms. Kay?"

"I think Dr. McCubbins is correct. No clear evidence he was in love with Ms. Cavanaugh. But, psychologically it was possible. Long-term and close working relationship. Dependence. Total trust. Partners. She was attractive. Sounds almost like a marriage."

"Suppose you're right! Which way does it cut in terms whether he murdered her?"

"Mr. Koger, is it?"

"Yes."

"We know there's a disheartening amount of domestic violence. Seems like there's a report of it happening every day in the news. Unfortunately, if he was in love with her, for me it cuts both ways."

"Can you explain that, Ms. Kay?"

"Husbands have murdered their wives for far less causes than the betrayal, ruin, and, I would say, infidelity Ms. Cavanaugh caused Mr. Truitt."

"Infidelity, Ms. Kay? Where does that come from?"

"We heard that she had sex with Gotti to buy time. Truitt seemed to wince when that came out in court. You could read it as a further, final betrayal. Particularly devastating if he were in love with her and didn't know it until he found out about Gotti."

"So, Ms. Kay, you're saying he killed her in a jealous rage?"

"No. I'm not. The other side of this, is what if he were in love with her? And it only dawned on him when he found out she gave herself to Gotti because he had power over her due to her debts and fear? He could feel sorry for her. Invoke his sympathy. If that were possible, he would not be able to kill her in such a brutal way.

Humiliating her and making her suffer a slow and agonizing death in that freezer."

"George Stevens here. My vote was 'guilty of a lesser offense.' If Truitt was in love with Cavanaugh, then my view is he killed her in a jealous rage. Betrayed not only financially, but emotionally, he lost it. Would you agree, Ms. Kay?"

"It's possible. But I have not reached your conclusion. I remain undecided."

"I'm Michelle Lasner. I voted 'not guilty.' I don't see Truitt as the killer. Admittedly, it is a confusing situation. But, I can't get around several factors. First, the murder was done in gang-land style. Gotti had to send a message to keep others in line, and hence, used the freezer.

"There's the testimony that Gotti bragged about getting off because of his connections. Then there's Detective Thornton's previous relationship with Gotti, causing him to be investigated for tampering with evidence. And although he was cleared, the fact remains that Gotti got off in that case. In this case, Thornton arrests Gotti and charges him with Cavanaugh's murder only to change his mind and charge Truitt. Part of his change of mind was the Buy-Sell agreement. But Truitt would not collect if he caused Cavanaugh's death.

"I don't see how you can conclude that a man with a criminal record, a record for violence and gangster activity didn't commit a brutal murder in the typical fashion of a mob hit. Then conclude that a man without any criminal record—and having no record of any violent behavior—brutally and viciously murdered his partner."

"I'm Mary Josephson. I agree with Ms. Lasner. I voted 'not guilty' as well. And I have a question about one of the jury instructions."

"What is that?"

"We're instructed that to render a verdict of murder in the first degree, the prosecution must prove the defendant caused Ms. Cavanaugh's death. That is, she would not have died but for the defendant's conduct. Also, that it was the defendant's conscious objective and purpose to cause her death. As I understand these instructions, it means we must find that the defendant intentionally forced Ms. Cavanaugh into the freezer without any clothes on. Then left her there, knowing she could not open the door."

"Your point, Mary?"

"I can't believe she just let him, whomever it was, the defendant or Gotti, just force her into the freezer. She would have fought to stop him. If she did, it would seem like he would have had to strike her or push her. But there were no signs of a struggle resulting in her being hit or pushed down."

"Haven't had my turn yet. I'm Charles Hudgins. I voted 'guilty.' Let me try and respond to Ms. Josephson's point she just made. Then, I'd like to address Ms. Lasner's points.

"I think Ms. Josephson may have a point. But, I'm not sure how relevant it is. That is, her point, I think, is that Ms. Cavanaugh may have been unconscious when she was put into the freezer. We heard that her DNA showed she had been drinking. So, the defendant got her drunk, or she got herself drunk or high. She takes off her clothes to seduce Truitt. Or Truitt takes advantage and gets her to remove her clothes to have sex with him. Afterward, she blacks out. He picks her up. Carries her to the freezer. Lays her down and exits, leaving her to freeze to death."

"It's a plausible scenario, Mr. Hudgins, that suggests an answer to my question. But the same scenario applies if Gotti was the murderer."

"You're right, Ms. Josephson. But hear me out. First, I believe in those that enforce the law. In this case, Detective Thornton and

Commonwealth's attorney, Audrey Payne. By that I mean, I don't accept that those with their background and experience would make such a huge mistake of choosing not to prosecute a known hoodlum and instead prosecute a businessman who had never been in trouble. This leads me to Ms. Lasner's analysis.

"The murder was indeed gang-land style. But, as the prosecution pointed out, that served as a perfect cover for Truitt. Cavanaugh's death gets him $500,000. Enough to restart his business. But he knows he won't get the money if he's connected with her death. But he also knows about Gotti. If Gotti is found guilty, Truitt is home free. Gets his $500,000. All he must do is make it look like a mob hit. It wouldn't take being part of the mob to think of using the freezer as the means to kill Cavanaugh. And he knows, or could figure out, that freezing her to death would make determining who the murderer was more difficult. Close to being the perfect crime—or should I say, crimes. Because by killing Cavanaugh and framing Gotti, Truitt also was defrauding the insurance company."

"As foreperson, I have this comment. The various positions asserted just now are well reasoned and well stated. Unfortunately, they lead to conflicting determinations and in some cases, no determination. To find the defendant 'guilty as charged,' 'guilty of a lesser offense,' or 'not guilty,' our verdict must be unanimous.

"Clearly, we are far apart at this stage. Having heard the arguments, we can take another vote. Unless you all prefer to continue the discussion. If so, before we resume, we'll take a break so each of us can review our positions. My own reaction is that very few of us, or possibly no one, has been persuaded to change his or her mind.

"If we do not come to a unanimous decision, we can inform the court that we have been unable to reach a decision. But, be aware! The court is likely to instruct us to try again. Judges are very reluctant to accept that we have become a hung jury. It means the prosecution has to decide whether to retry Mr. Truitt or let him go. In terms of our community, our inability to reach a decision means that this horrific crime remains unresolved and unpunished. It means that a vicious murderer, whether that is Mr. Truitt or Mr. Gotti, remains among us all.

"On the other hand, an innocent man could be convicted while the real murderer goes free and remains at large."

"My comments are not intended to change the positions of any of us. As the court admonished, each of us must stay true to our own analysis and convictions unless properly persuaded to change. With that, let's take a break. When we return, we can take another vote."

***

Dear Reader:

It is up to you to decide on a verdict. You may keep that to yourself or you can access my website www.hhcharles.com and record your vote. The status of the verdicts will be posted from time to time. You are invited to provide a brief statement of your reasoning for your verdict.

H. H. Charles

ABOUT THE AUTHOR

H.H. Charles is a pseudonym for Charles H. Helein, a practicing lawyer in Washington, D.C. His works are based on his experiences practicing law and living in the D.C. area. His first novel No Escape: A Maze of Greed and Murder covers the personal and political fallout of a proposal to legalize drugs. His follow-up work Dark Corridors: A Labyrinth of Loss, Lies, Lust, and Murder is based on true events on how big business gets its way in Washington through money, influence, cover ups, and murder. His third book Seeds of Anarchy: Crime of Indifference focuses on gun violence, its victims, and the proper scope of "the right to bear arms" under the Second Amendment. His fourth book, Book of Daniel follows a controversial vote from a State Supreme Court regarding the death penalty. His fifth book, You the Jury, delves into a court case for second degree manslaughter. It is up to you to decide the defendant's fate.

www.ingramcontent.com/pod-product-compliance
Lightning Source LLC
Chambersburg PA
CBHW052259220526
45471CB00001B/411